Parents, Please Don't Sit On Your Kids

A Parent's Guide to Nonpunitive Discipline

Clare Cherry
Director, Congregation Emanu El Nursery
and Elementary School,
San Bernardino, California

Photographs by Sam Cherry

David S. Lake Publishers
Belmont, California

Dedication

This book is lovingly dedicated to the memory of Rose Cherry, whose extraordinary compassion continues to inspire all those who knew her.

ISBN–0–8224–5307–X

Library of Congress Catalog Card Number: 84-61320
Printed in the United States of America
10   9   8   7   6   5   4   3   2

Contents

Introduction

It's 5:25 P.M. Kathryn Johnson has arrived home from work and has started dinner. David Johnson pulls into the driveway with Debby and Paul, having picked them up at their extended daycare center. Debby runs into the house, throws her things on a chair, takes a pillow from the sofa, and throws the pillow on the floor. Then Debby turns on the television, flops on the pillow, and rests her chin on her hands as she watches her favorite program. Her mother yells from the kitchen, "Turn off that TV and get in here! Can't you even say hello to me?" Then Paul comes running into the kitchen, sticks his hand in the salad bowl, and pulls out a cherry tomato, saying, "Mmmm, I love this kind of tomato." His mother grabs his hand and slaps it hard; the tomato slips out of his hand onto the floor. Mr. Johnson strolls in through the back door, carrying clothes which he picked up at the cleaner's on the way home. "Hi, honey," he says cheerfully. "I'll change my work clothes and come in to help you in a minute." Just then, he slips on the tomato and falls to the floor, scattering the dry-cleaned clothes all around. First, Mrs. Johnson screams at Debby, "I told you to turn off that TV!" Then she helps her husband up and asks if he is hurt. "No," he mutters. But as he collects himself and the scattered clothing, he begins to feel angry and shouts, "Damn it, it would be nice if just once we could have some peace and quiet around here. Turn off that TV in there like your mother told you to. Do you hear me?" Turning to his wife, he shouts, "She doesn't listen to anyone anymore, does she?" His wife is preoccupied. She grabs Paul and begins to shake him by the shoulders. "Now, see what you've done? Just because you have no manners, Daddy could have broken his leg!" She swats him vigorously two or three times on the seat and says, "Get in there and wash your filthy hands. And if I ever see you sticking your hands in the salad bowl again, you'll be sorry. Go to your room and stay there until dinner."

It's 5:45 P.M. now. Kathryn Johnson is feeling a little remorseful about spanking Paul. Having vented some steam, she's calmer now. She walks into the living room. "Debby, dear," she says sweetly, "if you turn off that TV and wash your hands, you can come in and help me with the whipped cream. You may even lick the bowl if you like." From the bedroom, Mr. Johnson listens to how his wife is speaking to the children now. He doesn't understand the change in her tone of voice.

At work, the Johnsons are both very good at supervising others. But they often leave their supervisory skills behind at the office. At home, they forget to be calm and consistent. It seems as if their kids never know what to expect. One minute it's the carrot and the next minute it's the stick.

Part I

Discipline:

Problems of Control for Children and Parents

CHAPTER ONE

Discipline from the Child's Point of View

Like all human beings, children need to receive love and to give it. Fulfillment of their physical needs alone will not ensure or maintain quality in their lives. Regardless of age, the inner self cries out for nurturing.

We adults, amid the complexities and concerns of our own lives, often forget that children are individuals with feelings and thoughts of their own. We have our own plans and desires, among which are preconceived images of how our children should fit into our families, schools, and social systems. As we get caught up in the maelstrom of our daily lives, too often our children are just swept along.

For children to enter into and be accepted in the world of grown-ups is, at best, a difficult task. The addition of discipline and punishment to their lives adds to the stress of their struggle.

How Children See Things

Children have their own ways of describing their lives. To check my perceptions and to hear their ideas, I interviewed 75 children, ages four through eight. I asked each one, "What is it like being a child?" Following are some representative responses.

> **A girl, age six:** I like going to school, learning to write, going out to play and skating, riding the bus to school, and riding my

bike. I would like to be seven years old. I don't like to be little, because then I can't be boss.

A girl, age eight: I'd rather be about thirty so I can be in charge.

A boy, age six: It's tough! Sometimes I'm forced to eat my cereal. Sometimes you have to get a spanking when you're a kid. Sometimes it's dumb being a kid because everybody thinks you're dumb. Sometimes it's great because grown-ups have to do all the work and kids get to have fun. The worst thing about being a kid is teachers won't ever listen to a kid.

A boy, age five: I would like to be very little so I could go into tiny places and someone can't find me when they're mad.

A boy, age five: Being a child is getting to play all day and don't have to do any work, and also since I am a child I don't have to watch my baby brother. But I have to watch him if they tell me to. I have to do what they tell me all the time. They always yell.

A boy, age six and a half: It's great because you get to do different things like going places or playing baseball. You don't have to worry about paying bills or going to work. Big people tell you what to do sometimes when you want to play.

A girl, age five and a half: I'm not a child. I'm in kindergarten. You learn about things, but sometimes the teacher gets too mad.

A girl, age eight: Boring. There's nothing to do because I can't do what I want to do. I wish I'd grow up tomorrow. I like to do the things my mom does, but I'm too little.

A girl, age four and a half: Children have to do what everyone tells them.

A boy, age four and a half: Sometimes children get spankings. That can hurt.

A girl, age four and a half: Sometimes children get spanked for nothing.

A boy, age four and a half: You get bossed a lot. The runaround system. "Go ask your father." "Go ask your mother." That's all I hear. And they yell a lot.

A girl, age six: Hand-me-down clothes. The oldest gets to go first. The youngest gets to be spoiled. I'm in the middle, and I don't know what I get to do. But I get to play and eat hamburgers and ice cream. I like to go to school. I like to put my hands in paint. Grown-ups don't like that. They get mad. They want you to be clean all the time.

A boy, age four and a half: Children can't do everything they want to do. They're always being bossed around and forced to do things they don't want to do.

A girl, age five: You have more fun and learn things. But you get bossed. Sometimes they don't smile. But they love you.

A boy, age five: Big people can yell and push you around because you're just little and you can't grow up very fast. When you're left home with a baby-sitter, you don't have much fun.

A girl, age five: Grown-ups get to go everywhere. Kids can't. Grown-ups decide for them. You can't do nothing.

A boy, age seven: Being a kid is hard when you have older sisters with boyfriends and your mom likes other people's boys, the way they act, better than you. She doesn't yell at them.

A girl, age seven and a half: The nicest thing about being a kid is what you do with parents when they are nice. But they're not always nice.

A girl, age seven: Being a kid is terrible. People are always telling you what to do. Sometimes they yell. Adults have no respect for you.

A boy, age nine: It's OK. But when your parents get a divorce you don't want to be a child. But I have fun, I guess.

Overall, the children who were questioned seemed to appreciate childhood and the importance of play. Most of them seemed to know they were loved. But they also seemed to feel that there was a conspiracy by the adult world to prevent them from doing what they want to do when and how they want to and are best able to do it. It seems obvious from the responses that children feel put down by, subservient to, and less significant than adults. Aside from play, the main themes running through the children's replies are desire for more control of their lives and feelings of fear and resentment toward angry, yelling adults.

Control in Children's Lives

Control of our children's behavior begins with our efforts to regulate their basic natural functions, such as sleeping, eating, and toileting, during the first two years of life. These efforts often produce tensions and antagonisms that carry over into other areas of our family life and erupt as conflict in minor incidents completely unrelated to these functions. Patterns of conflict may affect our attempts to regulate other areas of development, such as language, socialization, and motor skills. Conflict, then, can interfere with a child's development.

By age two children begin to develop a sense of self. They pepper their language with loud, emphatic *no*'s, challenging the control we exert. This sense of autonomy grows until children are about three years of age, when self-determination becomes a key factor in their lives. We need to allow them to experiment and explore to find out exactly what they can and cannot do to express themselves within socially acceptable limits.

Gradually, as children reach the age of seven or eight, the need to control their own lives becomes an even greater force. They want to be able to choose things to do that interest them and that they do well. They want to avoid being made to do things they can't do well or that create feelings of self-doubt and inadequacy.

With each new stage of a child's development, the potential for conflict with the parent is renewed. As parents, we must acknowledge children's growing drive for control. And we must come to terms with our own desire to control. As adults, we can reduce the potential for conflict. We can create home environments and develop systems of personal interaction in which our children have real opportunities to help determine the course of their own daily lives. We can develop attitudes within ourselves that convey to children, "I know you would like to be in control of your own life but, for your health, safety, and growth, there will be times when we will need to work out those controls together."

When we let children know that they will be given options whenever possible, they will be more cooperative in situations that allow them no choice. Parents can give children options and develop an ability to make choices. Parents can include children in decision-making discussions. In general, parents can help children to develop the skills needed to make plans and follow through on them.

Children need encouragement—and lots of patience—from us: It takes a long, long time to grow. However, in trying to help them develop independence, we become involved in power struggles and, thus, we often cause them—and ourselves—unnecessary tension. And in the eyes of the children, we often become angry, yelling parents.

Angry, Yelling Parents

Wittingly and unwittingly, we convey anger and disappointment to children in our most commonplace interactions with them. They are anxious to please us and really want to do things right. But instead of giving them the support and encouragement they need, too often we reprimand children with put-downs and punishments. Indeed, there seems to be a growing trend toward stronger and stronger control over the behavior of children, by the use of positive as well as negative methods—but control, nevertheless.[1] Perhaps this trend grows from anxieties and problems in our contemporary adult lives.

Today parents suffer uncertainty, fear, and tension about the future. Until recently, American life followed a predictable pattern: school, job, marriage, and then home and family. Since the sixties, factors such as social upheaval, out-of-control inflation, and simplification of divorce procedures have created new patterns of living, mating, and child-rearing. New anxieties about drugs, sex, crime, and unstable family life have developed. The single-parent family situation provides even more problems and anxieties. Confused by shattered traditions and the search for immediate solutions, parents are caught up in the vicious circle of trying to change their children instead of changing the conditions that pose the real threats.

The conscious and unconscious anxieties that grip our society have created a condition of mistrust toward the future and toward our children's potentials. We mistrust their—and our—abilities to cope with the rapid change that characterizes modern life. Our frustration and anxiety show in the interaction with our children. We may inadvertently threaten, humiliate, or become angry with them. Lacking trust, parents deny their children the opportunity to make choices freely and to learn of the many options that are available.

Children are very sensitive to even the most minor threats from grown-ups. They are sensitive to anger and yelling even when it's directed at another child in the family or to one or another of the parents. They see any kind of physical control as abusive and raising of the voice in anger as yelling and screaming. They are especially concerned with unfairness and impatience.

What Do Threatening Measures Accomplish?

In discussing punitive discipline, I am not concerned with the parent who has an occasional bad day. I'm concerned with the common adult beliefs that it is all right to yell at kids (especially if they are our own children), that it is all right to physically harass them, and that it is all right to hurt their feelings. Such methods are not all right; they are inhumane. They make our children feel humiliated, overwhelmed, and powerless. Such methods instill fear, they make children feel like failures, and they fail my test of what I call "mutuality," or the Golden Rule of Awareness:

> What I want for myself, I also must want for you; what I want from you, I also must be willing to give.

While threatening measures may temporarily solve an immediate problem for a parent, they do not improve children's behavior. On the contrary, they are models for a child on how to be an angry, yelling person who humiliates others. Remember that our children are our mirrors. They learn to treat others the way we treat them. Children will learn positive behavior from models of positive behavior and discipline. But if children are made to feel that they are genuinely bad, they may act bad accordingly.

Children usually will live up to and perform according to your expectations, even if you expect their behavior to be bad. Children who have been hurt and frightened may freeze up, lowering their own expectations of discovery and success, in order to stay out of the line of fire. Or they may do just the opposite. If they have been made to feel that you are their enemy, they'll fight. That's what enemies do. They will imitate the harsh disciplinary behavior you display, both in their relations with other adults and in conflicts with other children. Such conflicts often will be with children smaller and more helpless than themselves, again modeling the behavior you have demonstrated.

Some children have enough innate strength of character and self-esteem to withstand a parent's irrational or immature behavior. They may gain support from the other parent, another adult in the family, or an older sibling. The additional support may be enough to help the child counteract the deleterious effect of a nagging parent. Children may so develop their powers of creativity and imagination that through dramatic play experiences they are able to work out the negative feelings that a parent has instilled and to rediscover their own worth. If they have learned to recognize their own emotional reactions and have achieved some control over them, they will be able to withstand the onslaughts of your overreactions.

We tend to raise our children the way we were raised. And we tend to treat our children the way our own parents treated us. If we are caught in a pattern of hostile interactions with our children that is tearing at our self-respect and self-confidence and love, or if we are having difficulty managing our own feelings, we need to reexamine our attitudes. Patterns can be broken. We can effect changes in attitudes toward the discipline of our children. We can get away from the notion that it is all right for grown-ups to physically or verbally abuse children who are one-half, one-third, or even only one-fourth their size.

Our children are with us for only a small part of their lives. Their years of childhood are brief. They should be years filled with wonder and the beautiful magic of play, of growing, of knowing, and of love. We need to listen to what our children are saying. We need to give each fleeting moment serious consideration and know that we can help improve the quality of their lives by seeing them as the feeling, thinking, vital persons they are. We need always to try to understand them and to respect them. By doing so, we enrich our own lives and society as well.

Reference

[1]Clare Cherry, *Trends in the Use of Behavioral Control Methods by Parents of Young Children.* Redlands, CA: University of Redlands, 1979.

CHAPTER TWO

Discipline from the Parent's Point of View

It is an ongoing struggle to try to understand the points of view of children. We can give them life, live with them, love them, read books about child-rearing techniques and practices, and keep up with all the current research about childhood, but we still are forced to interpret our findings from our own individual point of view. Our conclusions and interpretations are based partly on knowledge of what already has been found to be true (by ourselves or by others), partly on what is taking place daily in our lives with our children, and partly on our personal beliefs. From these interpretations and conclusions come our hopes for or despair about the future of our own lives and our children's.

In addition to all of our studies and beliefs and intentions, we must acknowledge some basic facts about child-rearing. Young children need guidance to achieve self-direction, they need supervision to learn to live freely, and they need rules and limits to learn self-control. Their capacities for true autonomy, depending on their ages and rates of growth, are either latent, lagging for their age, or in the process of normal development. We are the ones who must help them in this process. By our sensitive guidance and perceptive supervision, and with our innate awareness of their need for protection, we must help our children learn to become free, integrated individuals. We have the responsibility of guiding our children to create a society that is more socially responsible and more reasonable than that which we know. We must model for our children the enlightened use of our intelligence,

the courage and strength to effect change, and the validity of caring for one another.

Goals of Discipline

The word "discipline" relates closely to the word "disciple": It connotes that the person being disciplined is learning to emulate the person doing the disciplining. We need to examine the effects of any discipline we use as well as our motives for using it. If our real motive is to demonstrate authority, superiority, and power, then discipline for its own sake is more important than the children being disciplined. If we believe that our children can achieve growth only through a strict system of reward and punishment, then discipline is merely a system for filling our children's minds with data and fear. We need to ask ourselves what our children ultimately will learn from our use of discipline. Will they learn that children should be seen but not heard, follow but not lead, be informed but not think? Will they learn to value submissive, subservient, blind obedience to any authority for its own sake?

How can we help our children learn, instead, to evaluate and make choices, to be considerate and fair in solving problems with others? We need to ask ourselves if our children should be punished for not yet knowing how to make wise judgments. We need to be sure that we use humane methods of helpful discipline so that our children may develop their own problem-solving and decision-making skills. Our aim should be to convey, through the disciplinary methods we use, such basic human values as respect, trust, honesty, and caring for others.

Our Mixed Emotions

The goals of parents are high; the responsibility is heavy. To get a perspective on how others handle the difficulties of this demanding role, I talked with many parents. Here are some of their comments about their good and bad feelings in connection with the behavior and discipline (or lack of it) of their own children:

> **Mother:** I love her so much, but I know I have to swat her on the butt to get her to do anything I want her to do.

Father: All I can say is, one child is enough. All she does is whine and cry and say "No!"

Mother: He's very good; I can scarcely believe my luck. But I'll tell you something: when his father tells him to jump, he'd better do it or else! We believe in strict discipline.

Father: I was spanked a great deal when I was a kid, and I made up my mind I was going to treat my own children differently. But I'm always screaming at them, and I know they must hate me at times.

Mother: I try so hard to do all the right things, but I get nervous and upset very easily, and there are so many problems. I just don't have the patience. I'm beginning to think I should never have had children. I wonder if I'm a child abuser.

Parents: Well, we're a very religious family. And we let our children know that God will punish them if they don't stay in line. We have very strict rules. When they break the rules, they certainly are punished. But they know that's because we love them so very much. They've learned that the more it hurts, the more we love them. We don't pull any punches.

Father: Well, I don't believe in spankings. But I'm desperate. My children never listen to me.

Father: I have enjoyed being a parent. I just live for my children. But I get so nervous when they start acting bratty and I don't know how to control them.

Mother: We talk things over a lot. Then when they don't listen, I just give them a good smack. I feel all worn out.

Mother: I've been lucky. My children are well behaved. We talk a lot. I do have to punish them to help them learn, but I never hit.

Father: I try to be fair and treat them the way I like to be treated, but when I come home from work, I get nervous and take it out on them. There's too much to do. I'm always exhausted.

Father: I love my boy so much. When I pick him up at school every day, my heart goes out with my love, as if I were seeing him for the first time. But he gets plenty of spankings. I was spanked as a kid, and just look at me—I'm OK!

Some of these comments probably sound familiar to you. They may even reflect some of your own emotions about being a parent. It helps to know that these mixed feelings are shared by others. You may gain a fresh perspective, though, from a sorting-out of these mixed-up feelings about the difficulties of parenting. Here is a breakdown of comments from some persons in my parenting classes:

For me, the hardest part about trying to be a good parent is

Keeping my cool

Finding time individually for each of my children

Not having time for myself

Following through on things I expect them to do

Having patience

Knowing the best way to teach values and behavior

Being consistent in my discipline

Not giving in to them because of my own laziness

Restraining my anger and desire to hit them when they misbehave

Not expecting so much of my children

The worst time for family harmony, especially with the children, is

Around mealtime

Before bedtime

When I first get home from work

When I'm getting ready to go to work

First thing in the morning, getting dressed

Evenings for me; mornings for my wife

Whenever someone is tired—it doesn't matter who

It seems like we're having hassles all the time

The parents in my parenting groups express great personal pleasure and satisfaction in being parents. They all feel that being a parent is hard work and carries with it the burden of overwhelming responsibilities along with the joys. Most of the younger parents speak of being very tired. Although most of the parents I talk with are enthusiastic, they also project an underlying current of despair. There is much concern about societal changes that so greatly affect their children's lives as well as their own.

The feelings of despair and helplessness are apparent especially when I raise the topic of discipline. Most parents lean heavily toward the use of physical punishment, but most of them also try to use humane methods of dealing with their children. Many are fearful of being too authoritarian, but all wish their children would not struggle so for control.

Personal Control

When parents are asked about discipline, it raises questions for them about themselves and their own capabilities. Discipline is something they feel they must resort to when things get out of hand—when they have lost personal control. Losing control of themselves is of special concern because, in the process, they lose sight of the goals of helpful, constructive criticism.

Usually the anger-causing behavior of our children is the catalyst for losing personal control. Anger interferes with judgment, and a lack of judgment in turn contributes to what may be an already deteriorating situation. Therefore, handling our anger is the first step in improving our skills in maintaining personal control.

Handling anger

In our discussions about anger, the adults in my parenting groups conclude that we manifest our anger in many ways. We get tense and display anxiety. We may bite our lips or grind our teeth. We may clench our fists or, if we get angry enough, we may even pound our fists on a hard surface or throw things. With some of us, our throats may start hurting or we talk louder and louder. Sometimes we may get nauseated. We get butterflies in our stomachs and a prickly sensation on our necks or arms, and we may start breathing heavily. We get backaches, shoulder pains, and headaches. But whatever we do, we do seem to need to express it.

Even those of us who are most skilled at controlling emotions need to express anger when we feel it. Anger is a healthy, normal human emotion. We don't seek anger: some occurrence causes the mind to act readily and develop feelings of anger. It is important to realize that it is the mind that makes the decision, even when we think we are doing something automatically. This is the first stage of anger, the cognitive stage. We may not have an awareness of anger building up during this stage, but it is there nonetheless.

When we become angry at our children, we may also be expressing feelings about other aspects of our lives. For example, when children fight with each other we may relate the fight to other problems we may be having in the home. We may feel guilty for not having taught the children better ways to work out a disagreement, and we become angry as a response to our guilt feelings. Or the fighting might stimulate an unconscious memory of having been a meek, nonbelligerent child and a disappointment to our parents, so anger may stem from that old embarrassment.

Just as we are all unique individuals, so we are also part of the human family, sharing universal traits. Part of our commonality lies in our bodily functions. Anger, which originates in the mind and which we may or may not be aware of, causes certain physiological modifications to occur which, in turn, increase our excitement. This is the second stage of anger—the physiological stage—which gives rise to many of the symptoms discussed above. Our muscles become tense; increased respiration and accelerated blood flow may cause our faces and necks to become flushed; the hairs on our arms and on the back of our necks may bristle, heightening the effect of the tightened muscles in those areas; and perspiration increases. These physiological effects cannot be denied, and there may be other signs.

Prolonged suppression or repression of feelings can have adverse effects on both physical and mental health. Anger must be recognized and dealt with. I have outlined some steps for learning to manage anger in a healthy, productive manner. Following them will make you feel better about yourself as well as help you to model for your children the wholesome handling of anger.

Develop cognitive awareness. Learn to acknowledge the first feeling of anger when it is still in the cognitive stage, before physiological reactions have begun to take place. For example, when you realize that you are becoming annoyed with your children, try to limit that annoyance to the cognitive stage by admitting why you feel annoyed and, if necessary, verbally stating it. This is where self-awareness becomes important. If you honestly and sincerely want to expand your awareness, you will acknowledge major and peripheral annoyances in your personal life that may be reflected in your quickness to become angry with your children.

A good first step toward greater self-awareness and bringing professionalism to your parenting is to keep a record of incidents in which you find yourself becoming most angry. Combine this record with brief notes about your life in general. After two or three weeks, review your notes. You may discover clues to your hidden motivations for anger. There may be a connection to some other aspect of your life, perhaps even your job. You may find a pattern that occurs at a particular time of the day, month, or year. You may even be able to relate your quickness to anger to something as basic as hunger or fatigue.

Once you acknowledge that cognitive first phase of anger, you can often manage to deal with it then and there. You may decide that the incident isn't worth getting angry about. You may realize that it isn't really the child you are angry at, but something in your personal life. You may realize that what the child is doing doesn't warrant anger— that the behavior is due to normal curiosity or a misunderstanding or some other legitimate factor. When you can recognize the beginnings of anger, you often can manage to release that anger simply by stating "I'm angry" or "That kind of behavior makes me feel angry."

Develop physiological awareness. The second step in learning to control your anger rather than letting it control you is to become aware of your physical reactions. If you acknowledge these physical reactions as signals that anger is occurring, you can use them to control that anger. For example, when you feel your body becoming tense, you can recognize that tension and voluntarily increase it for an instant; then release it. This is the opposite of denying or suppressing tension. When you suppress tension, you activate other muscles in your body, usually muscles that are in opposition to—antagonistic to—the muscles that have already become tense. This creates inner antagonism. So when you find yourself biting your lips, gritting your teeth, or otherwise tightening your already tense body, increase the action consciously for an instant and then release it. If you do not release angry tension, it escapes on its own. You see it when parents shout, make insulting remarks, inflict unjust punishments, lash out physically, pick on nonmisbehaving children, or go to other extremes in order to "let off steam."

Express anger rationally. The third step in handling anger is to learn to express anger in a way that can legitimately and constructively enhance family life. Compare the following qualities of rational and irrational expressions of anger.

Irrational Expression of Anger	Rational Expression of Anger
Communicates only negative messages	Is a valid communication tool
Intensifies the anger in others	Lets others know how you feel
Replaces your anger with guilt, lowered self-esteem, humiliation, embarrassment, and other negative feelings	Relieves your own tensions and restores your emotional equilibrium
Degrades others by attacking character, personality, or lack of skills	Does not reflect on the character or personality of others
Models for children the irrational expression of anger	Models for children ways they, too, can express anger in a rational manner

Now compare the expressions of anger reflected in the following examples. Notice how the irrational expressions result in the child's feeling humiliated or degraded.

Irrational Expression of Anger

You make me angry. (The message is "You are in control of me, the parent. You have the power to make me angry.")

You've ruined my whole day, and you've upset the whole family. (The message is "You're not only bad, but you have power over me and everyone in the family.")

You kids make me so mad that I can't even think. You make me wish I'd never had children. (The message is "I am a weak person. You children are much stronger than I am. You can even drive me away from my responsibilities.")

You are a disgusting, horrible child who doesn't care about anybody. (The message is "Keep on being disgusting and horrible because that is what I expect of you.")

You dummy! You could have killed your brother playing with that shovel! Don't you know any better? I give up with you. (The message is "You are an unworthy child who may as well stop trying to please me because I have given up on you.")

Rational Expression of Anger

I feel angry. (The message is a simple statement of how you feel.)

I'm tired of asking you to stop that shrieking. The noise bugs me. (The message is a simple statement of truth: the noise bothers the parent, who is tired of asking the child to stop. It in no way demeans the child or the parent.)

When you kids don't do what I ask you to do, it really annoys me. Sometimes I get really irritated. (The message states simply that when the children don't listen to the parent, he or she gets annoyed and irritated.)

That kind of language offends me. It is inappropriate for you to use those words. (The message is simply that the parent expects the child to refrain from using inappropriate language.)

Give me that shovel. I'm really annoyed. Tools need to be handled carefully. They are definitely not for hitting. (The message is that using a tool as a weapon is inappropriate and can be dangerous.)

Irrational Expression of Anger	Rational Expression of Anger
You stupid fools. Pick up these books right now and don't you ever go near the coffee table again. (The message is, first, that the parent thinks his or her children are stupid, so they may as well do other stupid things in the future. Second, the children see their parent as a liar, since they know they will be able to go near the coffee table again.)	That infuriates me. We keep those books on the coffee table for people to enjoy. I'm so angry I don't even want to discuss it now. (The message is that the parent is angry about the misuse of possessions, but that there is no need to discuss it while being so angry. The message also expresses trust that the children will put things back and not be so careless with them.)

Notice that in the column for the rational expression of anger, the parent is using "I" messages. "I" messages let children know how you feel, not how you judge them or how you think they should feel. Throughout this book you will find numerous examples of "I" messages and other ways to express anger rationally.

Rational expressions of anger allow you to build and use an expanded vocabulary. In addition to saying "I'm getting angry," "I feel very angry," or "That makes me angry," there are alternative words you could choose. Try some of these:

aggravated	cross	furious	mad
agitated	disappointed	incensed	mortified
annoyed	dismayed	infuriated	offended
antagonized	displeased	irate	provoked
bristling	exasperated	irked	put out
bugged	fuming	irritated	sore

The purpose of an expanded vocabulary is to be specific in expressing how we feel. It's surprising that merely searching for a substitute for *mad* or *angry* can relegate the entire problem to the cognitive realm, where it belongs. Besides, finding alternative words for *angry* can become quite an interesting game. The variety of these feeling-expressing words will gain children's attention, and you'll be expanding their vocabularies as well. It will be a real delight to hear your child cool a fight with a brother or sister by saying, "Don't do that! I'm getting antagonized."

You always need to be aware that children are learning, growing people. They don't deliberately want to make you angry. The advantage you have is that you deliberately want to express how you feel.

Release tension as a means of relaxation. The last step in handling anger in a rational manner is learning to release tension as a means of relaxation. Popular methods in use today include yoga, meditation, dance exercise, body building, tennis, bowling, and golf. Exercise is one of the healthiest and most natural ways of relieving stress. You can walk, jog, or run—alone or with others, even your children. Rising early to take a brisk walk or a short run before starting your day can give you extra oxygen and increase your metabolic rate so that you start your day with energy. Even a walk around the outside of your house will help. The invigoration brought about by exercise can carry over into all of your daily activities. Exercise works best if you do it on a regular basis—not necessarily every day, but at least three times a week. The extra time it takes will be more than made up by the time you saved through the reduction of tension-producing situations with your family.

You don't need to wait until you're free of your day's obligations to relieve stress through physical exercise. Whether you are home all day or have a job away from home, if you've had an especially emotional morning and feel a lot of pent-up tension, go for a brisk walk before you sit down to eat your lunch. You'll be more relaxed and able to evaluate the morning's problems with greater clarity, besides benefitting from better digestion.

Hobbies have long been known for their recuperative effects. Hobbies such as gardening, carpentry, oil painting, sewing, knitting, or modeling with clay can greatly refresh the human spirit. As your eyes and hands get involved in an activity, many difficult problems may fall into proper perspective. Anger dissipates, and calm is restored. You should experiment and use the ways that work best for you.

Don't despair if you lose control. Despite your best intentions and your efforts to express your anger rationally, there probably will be times when you lose control. You'll find yourself shouting, berating your child for a real or imagined infraction, and meting out unfair punishment. But it is better to let one's frailties occasionally come through than to act like an automaton. When you make a slip and "lose your cool," you can say to your children, "I'm sorry I'm so upset and angry" or "I'm sorry that I shouted at you" or "I'm sorry that I lost my temper, but I really was angry at the moment." Later, you can say, "I'm not feeling angry anymore, so let's sit down and discuss the situation." If you demonstrate the art of apology to your children, you will find they will learn how to give apologies appropriately.

Sometimes you will not quite lose total control, but nevertheless you will feel your anger building up. This is a good opportunity to model positive management of anger by saying, "I'm too annoyed to talk right now. But I know I won't be so angry later on. I'll wait until I don't feel so cross. Then we can discuss what happened." Again, modeling such behavior can teach your children to wait until *their* anger is lessened before trying to settle differences.

Keeping expectations in perspective

Learning to express anger is but one of many areas of concern when approaching discipline from a parent's viewpoint. Many sources of stress—besides a child's anger-causing behavior—need to be handled. The reality of parenthood may include sleepless nights, unexpected expenses, anxiety over the need for child care, and effects from an unstable marriage or maybe from divorce. In addition, parents receive conflicting messages about how to raise and educate their children, and they probably also have to contend with interference by well-meaning relatives, friends, and neighbors. Another source of stress is parents' high expectations for children. People come into parenthood with high ideals. All parents want to do the right thing, to give the right kind of guidance, and to ensure that their children will be well behaved, bright, successful, and wholesome. All these factors add stress in the parent's life. A parent is expected to

- Maintain an orderly, wholesome household

- Be an expert on child health and nutrition

- Dress children to look as the ads tell you they should

- Maintain an atmosphere of civilized cooperation

- Know what is needed for the achievement of preacademic and, later, academic skills

- Teach children to demonstrate socially acceptable behavior

- Know how to be a counselor and arbitrator

Parents will do well to keep self-expectations in perspective. Knowing that neither you nor your children are superhuman is a commonsense approach to minimizing stress.

Being a professional

It is important that, as parents, you keep yourself in as good mental and physical shape as possible. That in itself can make the job of being a parent, and maintaining an orderly household, more pleasurable. The secret is to apply yourself to the job of parenting as you would to any professional position. In our complex society, being a parent takes planning. There are several steps you can take to assess your needs and to raise your level of parenting:

Keeping diaries. As mentioned earlier, record-keeping can be very helpful in the development of self-awareness. It can help to identify patterns in your life and in your behavior (and in that of other members of the family) which may be causing problems. Two main advantages of keeping diaries or records of your family life are: (1) you may be able to identify and dispose of many minor irritants before they become major ones; and (2) you can isolate irritants and take one problem at a time.

Keeping family records. Maintaining a good home file system of all family records, papers, bills, receipts, etc., can save you much stress and anxiety when information is needed.

Having family meetings. Plan time for sharing feelings and ideas with other members of the family. There should be some time for the parents to be alone to discuss feelings, plans, and problems; there should be time for each parent to meet with the children for the same purpose. These sharing sessions can be most productive when they concentrate on "I" messages and problem solving rather than on complaints and criticisms. Children need opportunities to talk about their worries, their concepts of what is happening in their lives and in the world, and their fears and feelings.

Managing time. Plan your time carefully. The adults in a family should use a date book to keep track of all family appointments, errands, responsibilities, and other data—just as they would in a professional office situation. Parents should allow some personal time for themselves—both together and alone. Single parents especially should allow themselves time for other adult contacts rather than spending all of their nonworking time with their children. Some personal time for the pursuit of hobbies and recreation is important to your well-being. Try to handle mail only once; answer mail the day it arrives. If you receive a lot of junk mail, paperwork can be facilitated by a large wastebasket.

Choosing priorities.　Evaluate your obligations and try to eliminate those that aren't important. Put your time and effort into the things in your life that matter to you—the things that have real meaning for your personal and family well-being.

Planning short vacations.　Even a day spent away from home can be a mental refresher, as long as you have planned your day so as to avoid overexertion. Several "overnighters" throughout the year can make the need for long vacations less crucial. Children need vacations, too. An overnighter can be a refreshing break even for them.

Getting plenty of rest.　Parenting, especially if you have a job outside of the home, is strenuous. Plan your days so that there is appropriate time for rest and relaxation.

Knowing your limitations.　No one can be all things to all people. Know your limitations and concentrate on doing well within them rather than extending yourself until you damage your mental and physical health.

A Child-Centered Environment

While bringing your personal lives into balance, it is also essential that you evaluate your home environment. Your home is also your children's home, and it's important to take into account their ages and sizes and needs in planning the use of space. Don't be afraid to turn things upside down and approach your household routines and arrangements from some new angles.

The physical environment

Consider how the atmosphere in your home may contribute to a child's stress. Get down on your knees and look around the house from your children's point of view. Are things too high? Do colors which seem to blend harmoniously from an adult's vantage point possibly clash from the child's eye level?

Is the lighting adequate but not so intense as to be overstimulating? Are the ventilation, heating, and cooling arrangements comfortable for small children? What about the humidity? Very high humidity can cause headaches and irritableness; too much dryness can cause lethargy; too poor a flow of oxygen can cause drowsiness and depression. Any of these can lead to poor behavioral activity on the part of all family members, but especially of the children.

Are the acoustics comfortable? Reverberations can be annoying and stress-promoting. Children who evidence much hyperactive behavior are often unduly sensitive to sounds. Reducing the noise level frequently results in decreased hyperactivity. Floor carpeting helps reduce noise. Wall coverings such as rugs, carpeting, or heavy fabric absorb sound. Thick drapes diffuse noise. Outdoor plants help diffuse street or neighborhood noises that may be disturbing.

Are the children's play areas and sleeping areas attractive and orderly? Are their belongings accessible? Are arrangements comfortable? Are household furniture and belongings arranged exactly the same year-round, or do they undergo continuous small, interesting changes? Small changes, such as a new picture, a change in placement of a table or chair, or a rearrangement of a grouping of plants, acknowledge our continuously changing world and lend a note of anticipation and novelty to our daily routines.

Other environmental influences. Other items you might want to evaluate in relation to reducing stress in the home environment are:

- Provisions for spaces to be alone

- Restfulness of areas for sleeping

- Balanced, nutritional meals; nutritional snacks available

- Minimized competition between siblings

- Opportunities for participation in family's plans

- Opportunities for making choices

- Tolerance for use of imagination, inventiveness, and curiosity.

Getting children out of corners. We have a tendency to put our children into "corners." We give them a shelf in the corner—out of our way. And then we are concerned because their things are all over the house instead of in that corner. Try giving your child the privilege of keeping a box of favorite toys and books right smack under the coffee table in the middle of your living room—or perhaps even on top of it. This says to your preschooler, "You are important." Parents who have tried this find that the toys and books do indeed stay in the box except when actually being used.

The type of environment the children live in directly affects their behavior. This is not to say that a pleasant, wholesome environment will preclude behavior problems, but it does mean that factors contributing to negative behavior will be reduced, enabling you to concentrate your attention on more substantial causes of the behavior problems.

Establishing trust and sincerity

Once you have assessed your personal needs and have reevaluated your home environment in terms of stress reduction for the entire family, you are ready to concentrate on enhancement of the interaction you have with your children. Trust and sincerity are the cornerstones of the approach I am suggesting; they become the catalysts for growth.

Children learn at a very young age to mistrust most adults, including their parents. By the time they are two years old, many children have been tricked, coerced, and cheated by adults. They have been bribed with rewards that were not given and promises that were never kept. They develop a feeling that it is safer not to trust than to be fooled again and again. They have learned that their parents don't always mean what they say and that they use little subterfuges and double-talk in the hope that their children will be confused and not recognize their insincerity. In the minds of our children, we give mixed messages, and sometimes those messages are just wrong. We say things are easy when they're really hard. We tell our children "You can do it" when they really can't.

How do you rebuild trust in children who have learned to mistrust? The first step is to show that you are going to trust them. Trust breeds trust. Start out with little things: "I trust you to put the toys back before dinner." "I trust you to hang up your coat." "I trust you to take only two cookies."

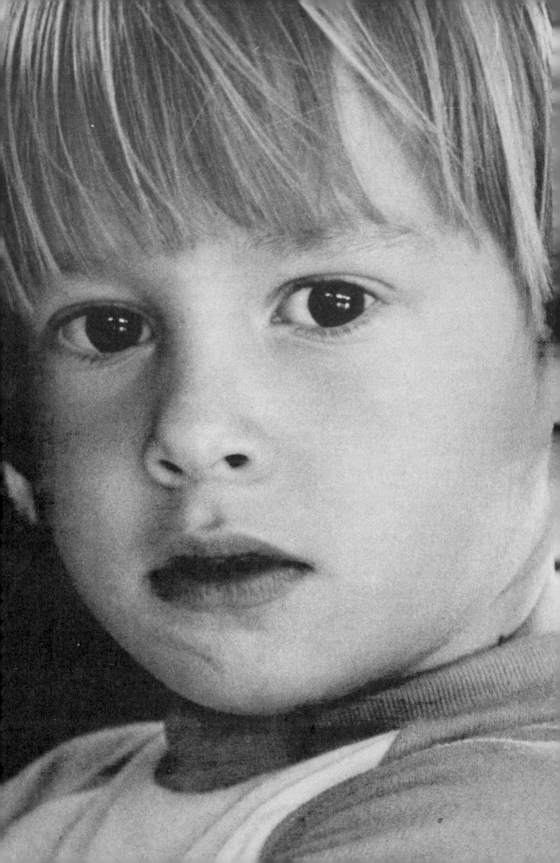

It takes courage to give real trust. We're so used to controlling our children by *if*'s ("If you don't do that right now, I'll give you something to remember!") that it is a complete turnabout to place faith in them. You can do so, however, by showing them continuously that they can trust you. They can trust you to do the things you promise to do, to be at the places you promise to be, to be on time, to give help when needed; they can trust you to be so involved with what they're doing that, by your interest, your presence, and your awareness, you protect them from losing control of their actions and their emotions. They need to be able to trust you to empathize with them when they are crying but not to probe and compound the issue by making them recount what happened. Yet they know that you are ready to listen, non-judgmentally, when they want to tell you what happened or why they are crying. They need to be able to trust you to allow them to fail, to give them encouragement when they want to try again, and to give recognition when they finally succeed. They need to be able to trust you not to have your expectations of them so high that they can't live up to them and to know that you don't expect them to be perfect.

Parents must be especially careful not to make promises that they can't keep, and to keep the promises they make. When an emergency or unforeseen circumstance prevents you from keeping a promise on occasion, acknowledge that fact and apologize for it. By the tone of your voice, your expression, your gestures, and your posture, you will impart sincerity and honesty, thus sustaining the increased mutual trust.

As you establish an atmosphere of trust and sincerity throughout your home, you can build on the warm, mutual feelings that result. In an atmosphere of trust, your children will explore their own individualities. They will not be afraid to be creative or innovative. They will develop awareness of their own uniqueness while appreciating the unity of the family group.

A trusting home is one in which there are rules for guidance and supervision. Young children need your help and protection; they need the security of knowing that you will set and maintain limits. But a trusting climate is also one that is open, honest, and caring. Attitudes are positive; the feelings of one another are important. Trust and sincerity are demonstrated by both verbal and nonverbal communication.

Communicating politely

Often, persons who are very polite and charming in their relationships with other adults fail to use the same mode of courtesy in their own homes. Parents frequently talk down to their children; they are rude, curt, and demanding in the requests they make of them. Then they become angry when their children talk back to them with the same lack of courtesy. It would be ideal if, as parents, we always spoke to our children in the same manner we do to guests in our home.

Here are some general rules of good communication which should be followed when interacting with your children:

- Always be sure you have the attention of the children to whom you are speaking.

- Say exactly what you mean, using words that are appropriate to the age and understanding of each child. For children of different ages, you may have to give separate statements to ensure that the youngest as well as the oldest understands.

- Enunciate clearly.

- Speak slowly and patiently. Modulate your voice so that it is low and gentle.

- Solicit verbal feedback, and look for nonverbal feedback. Don't go on until you're sure that what you said was comprehended. For example, say, "Tell me what it is I said to you," or ask, "What do you think I meant by what I said?"

- Listen to what your children say to you. If you don't understand them, help them to clarify it for you by repeating or rephrasing what they say. In other words, give them feedback. Don't rush them. Give encouragement. Reserve your response until you are sure you understand their intent. For example, "Are you saying that you get dizzy when you swing too high?" or "What you're saying is that you think your sister is selfish. Is that right?"

- Don't be judgmental. Don't base your response on predetermined conclusions, but rather on what is said to you at the time.

- Touch. Touching is an important form of communication, especially with your children. A gentle touch while you are speaking adds emphasis and will improve your child's ability to recall what you say or have said.

- Other types of nonverbal messages are also important, since nonverbal messages make up 93 percent of all communication between humans. Your demeanor and expressions should match your words so that you don't give conflicting messages. Again, use nonverbal messages as though your children were guests in your home. Nod. Smile. Lean slightly toward your children as you talk to them. Look directly into your children's faces rather than shouting from another room. Attend to your children when they speak; don't let your attention wander.

Good communication is demonstrated in the many examples given in this book. The principle is that what is being said and how it is being said—not the exact language being used—are important. Take note of this principle and practice your own natural ways of communicating messages. The ideal parent is able to sound assertive without being domineering or authoritarian. One way to add professionalism to your parenting methods is to practice your communication skills, just as if you were going to use them to make presentations to the public.

- Turn on the tape recorder some morning during the breakfast hour. Later, in private, play back the tape to hear how you sounded. It's even better to listen to it the next day; you can be more objective when you distance yourself from the experience.

- Practice talking to yourself while looking in the mirror, using the same expressions you use with your children. Then try to improve on what you hear yourself saying.

- Learn to differentiate between sounding *authoritarian* and sounding *authoritative*.

  This statement is *authoritarian*:   "I'm the boss, and what I say goes—right or wrong."

This statement is *authoritative*:   "I have had more experience than you've had, my judgment is better than yours, and I know the rules. I want to help you learn what I know."

Your children want and need you to be firm, knowledgeable, and assertive—as long as you are also kind, polite, and understanding.

Communication is largely a matter of feelings. When relating communication to discipline and behavior, think in terms of how your children are feeling at a given moment, rather than what kind of action they are performing.

Remember that by using "I" messages, you can let your children know how you feel about a situation without stifling their messages about how they feel. Don't try to tell them how they feel; open the door for them to communicate with you. You can help them expand their vocabularies for expressing feelings by using a variety of accurate terms yourself. Avoid ambiguous words, such as "*upset*," which might really mean *worried*, *embarrassed*, *impatient*, *frightened*, or *angry*. Don't settle for saying you feel "*good*," when you really mean *enthusiastic*, *challenged*, *relaxed*, *cooperative*, *festive*, *amused*, or *loyal*. Striving for accuracy conveys your own honest feelings as well as your respect for your children. Using these kinds of messages and words, you will soon hear them being used in return by your children.

In addition to talking about your own and your children's feelings, discuss the feelings of characters in traditional stories. For example, you might say:

"Do you know what really happened the day of the Three Bears story? Well, let me tell you about it. You see, the family overslept. The alarm clock didn't ring. That made everyone very nervous. Daddy Bear got very upset because they wouldn't have time to go jogging before breakfast. Mama Bear rushed so fast that she didn't watch where she was going. 'Ouch!' She stubbed her toe on the rocking chair. It hurt and she began to cry. Now she was really angry . . ."

You can add many more feelings as the story progresses. You can even add feelings to the stories you read. Then you might want to discuss them afterward, to help deepen your children's understanding. Gradually, as your children are able to identify more and more different kinds of feelings, you can demonstrate that it is possible to be in control of feelings instead of being controlled by them. You can model for your children the use of deliberate responses to specific feelings and the verbalization of them as opposed to reactive, emotional responses that are always counterproductive.

CHAPTER THREE

Reconsidering the Ways Children Irritate Their Parents

In struggling to develop independence, in wanting greater control over their own lives, in wanting people not to be angry with them, and in wanting to be acknowledged, children encounter great frustration. Their ways of expressing that frustration are often irritating to us. Misbehavior by children and the resulting exasperation of their parents and other adults is nothing new.

Misbehavior That Irritates Parents

A few years ago, I conducted a study in which I asked more than 100 adults between the ages of 18 and 75 what they remembered as the most common reasons for being punished when they were children.[1] I compared my results with those of similar studies of the same question.[2] The results of these three inquiries were amazingly similar. I assembled them into the general categories of misbehavior described in the following pages.

Disobeying rules

Disobeying rules includes not sharing, not taking turns, not following directions, and otherwise not responding socially as an adult would. Sharing and taking turns are social skills that our children have to learn. To become socially skilled, they need guidance, practice, and good examples from us.

Not following directions is a very common cause of conflict. You probably become exasperated when you find that your children are oblivious to instruction. If directions were limited to selected important tasks, however, they might not tune them out so easily. Adults have a way of going on and on:

> Well, go inside! Close the door, but don't slam it. Wipe your feet; hang up your coat; wait over there. I'll help you in a minute. Come over here; take this. Go wash your hands; you're really a mess! Comb your hair. We're going to eat—hurry up.

It's no wonder that children feel subservient to us. We communicate to them in ways that are degrading, unfeeling, and dehumanizing. How would you like to come home and have someone greet you with a string of commands and comments such as the above? They're not exactly rude, but they're a little overwhelming. Yet, in the onrush of our daily busyness and impatience, we often speak this way to our children.

If you don't communicate directions clearly and simply, your children probably won't respond. Then you become angry. Sometimes your directions may be clear but your children's perceptions may not be. You still become angry. Remembering, processing, and following directions is really hard for children in their developing years, even when they want to obey. Your task, then, becomes one of helping them to develop good habits of listening and responding. Simultaneously you need to develop your own good habits of listening and communicating: always remember that your children learn the behavior which you model.

Talking back and other forms of defiance

If your children are defiant, they are out of control. They need firm, compassionate help in regaining control. Clear, explicit requests, given with respect and geared to their respective ages, will be accepted more cooperatively than will demands that are shouted out in a domineering, authoritarian manner.

Disagreements may warrant discussion, but don't mistake an argument for a discussion. Arguments are confrontations in which people express opinions and feelings but don't listen to each other. They are, by and large, a waste of time. It takes two to make an argument so you need to learn to refuse to be drawn into them by your children. Discussions, on the other hand, are a valid means of communication. Basically, in an argument, the persons involved don't really listen to one another. In a discussion, all persons involved state their individual points of view, including what they think happened and how they feel. Each listens to the other. Even children as young as two and three years old can be introduced to the principles of discussion and can be taught to discuss their problems.

Fighting and other forms of violence

Children learn to use physical force by seeing others use it and by having it used on them by their parents, caretakers, and siblings. And they see a great deal of it on television programs and hear a great deal about it when adults discuss newspaper headlines. Our tolerance for violence in this nation is increasing dramatically, and it is our task— mine and yours—to try to let children know that there is also a world of nonviolence out there. Children do not generally want to hurt others. When young children use physical force, it is purely an emotional reaction and usually done without thought and without malice. Children respond well to being given alternatives to violence. Discussions can be encouraged. For very young children, you can simply state the facts for them. For example, you might say, "You can stop hitting Tommy right now. He doesn't like to be hit." Or you might say, "If you need to touch Tommy, touch him softly," instead of saying "Keep your hands to yourself." In other words, encourage friendliness by encouraging gentle contact. Meanwhile, you can say to Tommy, "Tell him you don't like that."

Being disorderly

I was one of those messy kids. No amount of nagging or coercion seemed to change my habits. Yet, I could be quite orderly when given no choice, and so can your children. When things need to be picked up, cleaned up, or put in a particular order, say exactly what is to be done and when. For example, "Kristy, put the paper dolls back in the drawer right now" is better than saying "Those paper dolls are a big mess." Instead of saying "Clean that stuff up before you come to dinner," you might say, "Your cars need to be put on the shelf before you come to eat. We're going to eat in a few minutes."

Parents frequently apply double standards when expecting neatness. I've seen children yelled at for leaving a sweater on a living-room chair, while Mother's shoes are under the coffee table and Daddy's are lined up next to the sofa. I have seen parents insist that children straighten out their play areas and the materials which they have been using, while the workbench in the garage looks as if a cyclone struck it and a big mess is accumulating on top of this morning's mess on the kitchen sink. Orderliness should be the responsibility of the entire family, working together. The same rules should apply to all, young and old.

Not coming when called

Children will come when you call them if they know that you mean it. I interviewed a number of children about the matter, and they told me that they know they don't have to come until the third, fourth, or fifth call. The number of calls depended on the child and the parent. When asked why, they all usually gave the same or similar response, "Because then she (or he) really means it." Those who said they come on the first call also responded, "Because I know she (or he) means it." So when you call your children, be sure to:

- Get their attention.

- Call only once.

- Say when you want them to come, such as "right now."

- Go get them physically (but not angrily) if they don't respond. Don't nag or lecture. Simply show them by your actions that from now on you intend to call them only once.

Sometimes a child hears the call but doesn't register what was heard. Then, you might try saying "I called you" as a sort of gentle reminder. It still falls into the category of calling only once, and it might avoid the need for physical reinforcement.

Sometimes you can give a choice, which gives your children important feelings of being in control. You can say, "I want you to come here right now. You can come by yourself, or I can come and walk with you, or I can come and we can hold hands while we walk." (Moving children along by cupping your hand under their elbow is a nonviolent, nonhurting reinforcer.) Because you already have demonstrated that you follow through with what you say, children will usually choose to come to you without physical help. Be careful not to give choices unless the alternatives really are acceptable, and never use choices as threats. If you take your child by the hand (or the elbow, as described above), do it gently but with sureness. Your goal shouldn't be to hurt your child or to demonstrate anger. You simply want to be sure that the child comes with you. Be confident that the next time, or maybe the next, the choice will be to come without your extra help—provided you haven't made a big deal out of it.

Courting danger

When your children's safety is at risk, the first rule is to remove them from the danger as quickly as possible. Don't worry at the time about right or wrong handling. Don't stand on ceremony—act.

If you have one or more children who repeatedly expose themselves to danger, consider that they are probably in great need of an extraordinary amount of adult attention. Try extra hugs and loving touches. Become your child's close friend. Give extraordinary amounts of reassurance. Build trust. Examine your schedule. Do you spend enough quality time with your children? Is your child one of those who is willing to risk even death in order to get busy adults to pay attention? Such children are willing to be at risk, having found it is a good way to make their parents sit up and take notice. You need to let them know constantly that they are important to you and that they don't have to take risks to get you to notice them. You can't tell them these things; you need to demonstrate them over and over again.

Set firm limits on specific risks. "You may absolutely not touch that switch at any time," or "You may play only on the sidewalk—never in the street," or "You need to come down from that roof right now. We have a rule that children are not allowed up there." These things need to be said with great emphasis but not as angry threats.

Television viewing creates a phenomenon in which children see many persons—sometimes children—taking risks. It is hard for young children to distinguish between what is play acting or fantasy and what is reality. It is important that you try to help them understand these differences.

Using vulgar language

This is an area where double standards run rampant. The language used by adults in many homes today is peppered with vulgar words and salted with sex-oriented phrases. Many parents ease up on the use of vulgarity in their language when their children start talking, but usually it is too late. The children have already heard many words used almost daily that were not considered acceptable household words even 20 or 30 years ago. Mores do change. But parents' desire for children to retain their innocence remains the same.

Even under the most wholesome of circumstances, young children enjoy experimenting with words, and such experimentation should be encouraged. But sometimes they begin experimenting with words related to toileting and, later, to sex. With two- and three-year-olds this can be largely ignored: If the words don't elicit shock, the behavior won't be reinforced. With four- and five-year-olds you can give explicit instructions: "Those words may not be used in our home," or "Our family does not use those words." Then be sure that they don't use those words.

Sometimes children will start insulting one another and exploring the use of many of the vulgar words and phrases you thought they didn't hear you say. This can be a time to sit down with your children and discuss openly which words are so unpleasant that they may not be used. Unpleasant words can be called *hurting words*, and you can explain that it hurts some people, or it hurts you, to hear them. Children are very sensitive to shock reactions and will go to extremes to get a reaction. Firm, precise rules about what they may and may not say are all that is necessary. Avoid reinforcing the undesirable language through nagging and punishing. The rules, by the way, should apply to the entire family.

Inappropriate sexual exploration

It's natural for children to be curious about one another's sexual organs, and they will often engage in exploratory play. There are several ways of dealing with such situations. But first you have to be trusting of the fact that it is normal to do so, that your children are not perverts, and that sexual curiosity is not dirty. With two- or three-year-olds, you can usually ignore their actions: if you don't overreact, this type of behavior usually stops. With four- to eight-year-olds you can say, clearly and without excitement, "You may not touch her vagina" or "You may not play with his penis." If the message is given clearly, it will be received clearly. Avoid nagging, making them feel guilty, or implying that body parts are dirty. And don't worry that your children will be sexual deviates. Instead, just clearly express your expectations to your children.

Having children of the opposite sex see each other naked when they are in their preschool years will often satisfy their curiosity for many years to come. There are many well-thought-out books written on sex education for young children. They will tell you of the appropriateness of using correct anatomical terms and phrases in the home. Often, telling children exactly what various sexual and anatomical phrases mean satisfies their curiosity and they have less need for sex play and talk. (Consult with your public library and local bookstore for recommended books on sex education.)

Lying and stealing

Preschool children have vivid imaginations and love to play make-believe. They frequently have difficulty differentiating between reality and fantasy and may need help in doing so. Sometimes children seem to be telling outright lies when in fact they are merely distorting: because they are young, they misunderstand what really takes place.

Sometimes lying is deliberate. It may be prompted by fear of punishment based on past experiences. As your children get a little older, they may get in the habit of lying to build their own egos, to make others feel jealous, to avoid punishment, or to gain your attention. Whatever their reasons, you should confront your children with their lies—unobtrusively to avoid embarrassment—and encourage them to practice telling the truth.

Unfortunately, most parents give their children many examples of "little white lies":

- I have to go to the store for ten minutes. I hate to leave you alone, but if anyone calls, tell them I'm in the shower.

- I don't want to talk to her. Tell her I'm taking a bath.

- Don't tell Daddy we were in this store. I don't want him to know what I bought.

- Don't tell your mother about our meeting Jennie. She might not understand that she's just an old friend.

- If someone from the bank calls, tell them I'm out of town and that a baby-sitter is taking care of you.

When adults model such behavior as these examples show, children see that it is all right to lie. You need to be scrupulously honest in front of your children and careful not to establish double standards.

Children who must be left alone for a short while should be taught to say over the phone, "My father (mother) can't come to the phone right now. Leave your number and he (she) will call you in a little while." This is a true statement and does not encourage your children to tell lies. If the person calling asks, "What are your parents doing?" or "Where are your parents?" your children should say, "You can ask them when they return your call." Tell them not to give any additional information. If the party questions the child further, the child should say, "I have to hang up now," and the child should hang up. If your children understand these steps, you will be helping to protect them, but you will not encourage them to tell lies.

Children sometimes develop a habit of taking things that belong to others, often to an older sibling or a playmate. With such children, you can simply say, "That doesn't belong to you. Give it back," or ". . . Put it back." Sometimes children who are obsessed with taking things furtively or who lie frequently need professional help to get at the root of the obsession. (See Chapter 11, "Systematic Problem Solving.")

Tattling

Some children acquire the habit of tattling when their own self-esteem has been diminished, when their own wrongdoings have been pointed out over and over, and when they have not been given constructive guidance toward more acceptable behavior. You can handle tattling in a way that will help your children learn new behaviors. When someone says to you, "Benji takes all the good crayons and gives me the broken ones," you can say, "Benji should share. Can we think of something that Benji does do really well?" You might get a response such as, "Yeah, he should share." Then you might say, "But what does he do that you like?" The answer might be "He ties my shoes for me" or "He can climb trees better than anybody." Thus, while acknowledging Benji's wrong actions, the discussion ends on a positive note, and the habit of tattling is not reinforced.

Meanwhile, it might be important to evaluate the relationship between you, your children, and other members of the family. Make sure that the tattler has a chance to build self-esteem and self-confidence. Also make sure that there isn't a real situation of one child continuously taking advantage of another.

Whining

Whining seems to be one of the most out-of-proportion irritants to parents, and yet it can be one of the simplest to handle. Whining develops into a habit because it gets attention. Sometimes it becomes a major issue with a child. You can usually take care of whining very simply by refusing to respond to it. If children are not ill or becoming ill, if they are not suffering from a speech impediment or other physical handicap that may affect the way they talk, and their basic needs are being met, you can just tell them in plain language that you will not respond to whining. Say, "I can't understand you unless you talk." In extreme cases you might say, "If you need to make that noise, please do it where I can't hear you. I don't like to listen to it." You could add, "I do like to hear you talk, though."

Whining probably stems from hearing parents speak in that special tone of voice, raised higher than the normal speaking level. Parents often develop the habit of speaking to their young children that way. Baby talk and other forms of artificially manipulated tones that an adult uses will be emulated by children and come out as whining. So it's important to examine your own way of speaking and make sure that you are modeling normal tones.

Temper tantrums

The temper tantrum, like so many other undesirable behaviors, is an emotional reaction to not being able to control. It is a powerful attention-getting device. You have to believe that temper tantrums will be eliminated when the attention they get is eliminated. When children throw tantrums, they should be left without an audience—either by all persons leaving the scene of the tantrum, or by removing the tantrum-thrower to a private place—not angrily, but with great firmness and purpose. Children who habitually vomit while throwing a tantrum will usually not do it again if once (sometimes twice) they are allowed to sit in their own vomit instead of having someone immediately rush to them, fuss over them, and clean them up. Even if your fussing actions are negative, they still are being controlled by the child—who revels in the resultant feeling of power.

Sleeping, eating, and toileting problems

These usually are problem areas for parents of very young children because of the parents' desire for children's early maturity and self-control. Parents often want their children's rate of development to conform to that of other children. We can't program natural biological and physiological functions, but we can show great patience toward our children and great tolerance for natural developmental patterns. Here are some helpful hints:

Sleeping. This becomes a problem because double standards are being displayed. Children usually go to sleep while their parents stay up watching television, entertaining, reading, talking, and doing all sorts of things that the children would like to do too. If your children have already acquired habits of not going to bed when told, make a checklist of all the kinds of excuses they use for not being ready to sleep. Here's a sample checklist. You may want to make your checklist into a weekly chart, giving stars for each item accomplished.

Sample checklist

Washing hands and face

Brushing teeth

Putting on pajamas

Putting dirty clothes in hamper

Laying out next day's clothes

Saying goodnight to everyone in family

Giving hugs

Giving goodnight kisses

Having a snack (should be protein, such as cheese or peanut butter, if child is a bed-wetter)

Having a drink of water (should be approximately 2 oz. if child is a bed-wetter)

Turning night light on, main light off

Reading one bedtime story

Patience, consistency, persistence, calmness, and assertiveness will eventually pay off in the elimination of bedtime power struggles. After you have completed the checklist, if your children get out of bed, they should be taken back to bed, quietly but firmly—without comment. They might be carried or just led by the hand. The important thing is to avoid responding to various manipulative pleas and maneuvers. Don't nag, scold, threaten, yell, or talk with them. All adults or older siblings should cooperate by totally ignoring the situation, although either one or two parents may be handling the checklist. Usually, three or four nights of such a pattern will establish better going-to-bed habits, provided consistency is maintained.

Eating. Children should eat according to their own appetites. As often as possible, try to offer the kinds of nutritious food for which they show a preference. Children should not be tricked, coerced, or nagged about consuming what has been offered. They should not be told what to eat first and second and so on. By recognizing that their appetites vary according to the children's rate of growth, and by not emphasizing the times they don't eat, mealtime will become less of a problem. Try not to reinforce the difference between your children's eating habits and those of adults. If necessary, to avoid being aggravated by your children's eating habits, it may be wise to feed young children separately from the rest of the family (preferably beforehand) for a while.

Toileting. Most of these problems stem from trying to rush children into toileting habits for which they are developmentally unprepared. It's important to recognize that some children, once they start becoming toilet-trained, will need many weeks, or even months, to achieve full control. Patience is important. To avoid reinforcing "accidents," it's important not to get upset or excited or give lectures and rules about when to go and when not to go to the toilet. If a child reaches the age of four and still has not achieved control, professional help may be needed.

Doing schoolwork carelessly

Personally, I was surprised that this behavior seems to bother so many parents. When a child does sloppy work, the natural consequence should simply be having to do it over again. Punishment should not be connected with the consequence. Your goal should be to help your children take pride in their work. Therefore, make sure if you ask your child to redo an assignment that you allow time for this. Avoid taking away the child's normal playtime. If necessary, rearrange your schedule so that appropriate time is available to help or supervise or provide motivation.

A child who continually does sloppy work may be suffering from a visual problem, poor eye-hand coordination, or another perceptual difficulty. Many children with mild perceptual problems are very sloppy in their work because they have difficulty judging the pressure of the pen or pencil or even the pressure of their own hands on the paper. They may have difficulty assessing spatial relationships. These are children who frequently drop things, spill things, bump into things, and otherwise appear to be clumsy. These children require special understanding, and they should be evaluated to determine the cause of such behavior. Whatever your child's problems may be, look for ways you can help rather than becoming angry about sloppy schoolwork.

Not participating

Some parents become angry when their children hesitate or flatly refuse to participate in various social or school functions. Rather than becoming annoyed, it may be helpful to try to find out what the problem is. Are your children shy? Do they feel that if they participate they will make fools of themselves because they can't perform as well as their peers? Do they feel they don't speak the language well enough or that their clothes aren't as chic as those of others? Do they want to participate but feel that they have no friends? Do they suffer from stage fright? Are they afraid of failing or of being punished? Have they been conditioned not to speak up when adults are talking or dominating the group? Can they hear and understand well? Can they see clearly? Are they uncomfortable because they're new in the neighborhood or class? Some persons simply need a long time adjusting to new groups.

Children who do not participate in social activities frequently need help in finding just one special friend. The years of four to eight are especially sensitive years for the development of social skills and the development of friendships. Social skills are progressive, as are other areas of growth. If children are not given opportunities to develop friendships at age four or five, they may show difficulty in doing so at ages seven or eight. Inviting young children of friends and neighbors into your home is a good first step in helping your own children develop techniques needed for making friends.

Children who stay clear of speaking in front of others may be helped if given opportunities to work with tape recorders. Hearing their own recorded voices and realizing, as a result, that they sound quite normal may help some children lessen their shyness. A child who has even a mild speech deficiency, however, may continue to be reticent about speaking in a group. Eventually, the speech deficiency may be corrected, or the child may learn not to regard it as a problem. Then, the child may cease being shy.

If you have a child who you feel is too frequently a nonparticipant, you may want to speak to the child's teacher or physician. Or you may seek other professional sources for assistance and recommendations. The reason for the child's nonparticipation is critical to the problem and its solution. A child's low self-esteem is often the issue. But the problem could be very different: a child may truly not be interested in the nature of the social or school functions available. Whatever the problem may be, parents must strike a balance between refraining from forcing children to do what makes them feel uncomfortable and gently exposing them to new experiences that will interest them and encourage participation.

References

[1]Clare Cherry, *Trends in the Use of Behavioral Control Methods by Parents of Young Children*. Redlands, CA: University of Redlands, 1979.
[2]R. Sears, E. Maccoby, and H. Levin, *Patterns of Child Rearing*. Stanford, CA: Stanford University Press, 1957; and L. M. Stolz, *Influences on Parent Behavior*. Stanford, CA: Stanford University Press, 1967.

CHAPTER FOUR

Reconsidering Why Children Misbehave

When we try to understand why our children behave the way they do, we often need to look past their behavior to factors beyond their conscious control. Particularly when our children continuously provoke discipline or punishment, great care should be taken to look for possible underlying causes. Some causes of behavior problems are explored in this chapter. You may find that one or more relate to your own children.

Why Most Children Misbehave

All normal children go through the same developmental stages, and most encounter similar kinds of social and family conflicts. These factors contribute to ordinary—and often predictable—patterns of poor behavior. A number of these "normal" behavior problems will be discussed here. Some extreme behavior problems and situations will be discussed at the end of the chapter.

Immaturity

So many problems with our children are simply due to immaturity. Each month of a child's growth brings an improvement in motor coordination, spatial awareness, ability to solve problems, ability to follow directions, and ability to interact socially with others. Often we place children in nursery school, kindergarten, or primary school only to discover that they are not quite as mature as most of the other children in the class. The resulting stress can lead to misbehavior both in the school and in the home.

Some children who are immature for their age need an extra three or so months to grow; some need another six months; some may even need an entire year to catch up. This doesn't necessarily mean that the child will always be less mature than others; rather, the child's rate of growth, though normal in sequence, may be slower than that of others. For example, a child may not be ready physiologically to learn to read until age seven, at which time he or she suddenly becomes the best reader in the class. Children who have slow rates of growth need to be protected from the daily trauma of being shamed and pushed into attempting tasks for which they are not developmentally ready. This pressure to learn produces unnecessary tension and may cause emotional scars that will never be totally overcome. This pressure also provokes negative behavior in other areas of that child's life.

Avoid making comparisons between your child and other children; refrain from rushing your children from one stage of growth to the next. Instead, learn to revel in their childlikeness and appreciate them as they are. All too soon they will become adults and develop independent lives of their own.

Boredom

Parents frequently use boredom as an excuse for the misbehavior of their children. Usually, however, there is more to apparent boredom than meets the eye. Children with visual or auditory problems often act bored because they are not taking in appropriate sensory information. They seem tuned out because they *are* tuned out. Children who are completely absorbed in their own thoughts may appear to be bored. They might be worried and depressed about a family crisis, real or imagined. They may be extremely jealous of a sibling. They may be worried about fears or about imagined problems with their own bodies. Children so gripped in an emotional vise are not able to relate normally to family experiences.

Children who have been placed in the wrong classes at a nursery or elementary school or other type of child-care or educational center may look as though they are bored. They may actually be bewildered because they are too immature for their group. On the other hand, children who are too mature may feel that they don't belong—and they don't. Such children may "turn themselves off" and daydream about other, more satisfying experiences. Daydreaming is very normal behavior for young children, and they shouldn't be faulted for it.

Continual criticism will cause children to put on a facade of boredom, which expresses the tenet that "it's better to be quiet and be thought dumb than to speak and remove all doubt." Gifted children sometimes need greater motivation than other children. They may be mentally brilliant or artistically talented but immature emotionally or socially. They may have set standards for themselves that are too high for them to meet. These children need your help in undertaking tasks for the joy of doing rather than for the purpose of achieving. Parents can see to it that they create enough motivation and opportunities for their children to find satisfying growth experiences on appropriate levels and with some degree of independence. This will help decrease the child's need to behave in a rebellious, antisocial, and nonconformist manner.

Curiosity

It is normal for your children to want to increase their understanding of the environment through exploration, experimentation, and questioning. These kinds of experiences occur during normal play activities, reflecting children's intense desire to understand their environment. Rather than restricting their curiosity, thereby causing stress, you should promote and encourage it. When curiosity leads them into difficulties, you must remember that they are in a process of learning. When your children are given legitimate opportunities to satisfy their curiosity, they probably need less behavioral control.

Visual and auditory disabilities

Very commonly, young children go for months or years with undetected auditory or visual problems. Such disabilities can cause great distress for children and, in turn, cause them to appear to misbehave. If you frequently feel that your children aren't listening, you should have their hearing checked. When you find that your children frequently bump into things and drop things, their vision should be checked.

Often children are reported as having 20/20 vision and normal hearing, yet the symptoms of visual or auditory disabilities continue. Even though these children physically hear and see well, they may be perceptually immature, not really processing what they see or hear the way others do. Frequently, this is merely a developmental problem and the children just need more time to grow. However, some children are so deficient that they should be given remediation exercises to increase their perceptual skills.

Much progress has been made in recent years toward defining the neurological relationship between perception, behavior, and learning. Learning takes place in the brain; perception occurs in the brain; movement is directed by the brain. Children who have difficulty with visual or auditory perception need a system of perceptual-motor training that will integrate the sensory information they receive with other brain functions, such as learning and movement.

It has long been known that developmental exercises such as crawling, jumping, balancing, climbing, hopping, rolling, and spinning can enhance perceptual-motor skills. But new brain research and new findings in the area of the importance of integrating the left and right hemispheres of the brain are opening doors to helping children achieve maximum developmental potential. If you suspect your child of having serious perceptual problems (that is, if the child continually bumps into things, has poor balance, or moves erratically or lethargically), you should seek appropriate sources of evaluation and remedy. Not all communities have such sources; you may have to do a little research. Some physicians will help you find groups that specialize in working with neurologically handicapped children. Some communities have clinics that specialize in perceptual-motor training. Some physical therapists and/or dance specialists can give help in perceptual-motor development or refer you to an appropriate resource. Don't despair; there are specialists in this important but not highly popularized field of development. Sometimes, just a little help from trained specialists will improve a child's perceptual abilities, which in turn will increase the child's self-esteem. This, then, will lead to improved social skills and emotional well-being.

Family crises

Your changing family conditions have a continual effect on your children. It's especially important that you remain alert to how changes in the home, job, or even your social life affect your children as well as yourself. Occasionally, an insignificant matter may be the cause of negative behavior on the part of your children. Children sometimes misinterpret adults' comments about minor issues and decide something horrible is going to happen. It is also most likely that your children are aware of major family crises that you think are well hidden from them.

When you know there is a problem affecting your children's personal lives, encourage them to talk about it. One technique for getting them to open up their feelings to you is shown in this example of a parent talking with a young child:

Parent: You seem very quiet. Do you feel sad?

Child: (no response)

Parent: Did someone say something to you that made you feel bad?

Child: I hate you.

Parent: You *feel* as if you hate me.

Child (picking up a hammer lying on a table nearby): I'm going to break the window.

Parent: You feel so angry that you're going to break our window.

Child: You like me.

Parent: I love you very much.

Child: Aunt Suzy is going to take care of me while you go 'way.

Parent: We're only going to be gone for a few days to help Grandma move. She needs to live where someone can take care of her. Then we'll be back home and we won't have to worry about Grandma so much.

Child: Aunt Suzy knows good stories. Can I go play?

Children may get great relief simply from having an opportunity to express their concerns. Talking about the problem may be enough to relieve their feelings or at least to put the issue in perspective. The important thing is to let them know that they have a right to their negative feelings and that they will not be punished for them. On the other hand, if they do not want to talk about it, you need to be understanding and hope that your extra care, attention, and patience will help lessen their inner turmoil. In such cases, they also need to be reassured that they will not be punished for not wanting to share their feelings with you. Such reassurance may give them the courage to open up a little.

In discussing family problems with your children, remember that adult explanations won't work. Try to see the problems from their point of view. For example, if a separation or divorce is pending, try to understand that your children see it as their separation or divorce, not yours. They cannot easily distinguish themselves from the family situation they have known. A death in the family—or even a situation such as an older sibling leaving home for college, marriage, or for some other reason—can be unusually stressful for children. Even moving to a new home can be a traumatic experience for young children, resulting in much negative behavior. Imagine the situation from their viewpoint; talking, listening, and being close to them will usually ease their stress.

Sensitivity to foods or environmental factors

In recent years much research has been done on the extraordinary sensitivity that some people have to ordinary environmental factors. Symptoms may resemble those of common allergic reactions, such as hay fever, or they may take the form of hyperactive behavior, in which case a vicious cycle can set in. Often, children so affected are subjected to repeated correction, criticism, confinement, or other methods of control. Yet, these children are physiologically unable to control the behavior, and punishment only aggravates the situation. Children build up tremendous guilt and may become convinced of being misfits. Misbehavior then becomes a reaction to others' expectations and finally to the children's own expectations, all of which are based on false assumptions.

Every effort should be made to find out why your children act the way they do, especially in the case of hyperactivity. When environmental factors seem to be a cause, the following simple plan may be successful:

1. Keep a daily diary of your child's activities. For each activity, list the time, place, and any unusual behavior. Take note of anything unusual in the environment, such as fresh paint or other chemicals, sprays, animals, or unusual odors.

2. Keep a similar diary for everything your child ingests; include a list of ingredients. Note the brand names of packaged foods. Half an hour after each meal and snack, note your child's behavior. An A to F rating scale can be used—A signifying the most acceptable behavior, F the least desirable.

3. After two or three weeks, study and analyze the diaries for connections between environmental factors and behavior and between diet and behavior. You may want to continue the process for up to six weeks for a more in-depth analysis.

4. If this method does not surface possible irritants to your child, professional help should be obtained.

Family behavior

By the time they are toddlers, young children have learned many variations in social and moral behavior by observing the behavior of family members, especially that of siblings. Sometimes the behavior is negative. It may include crying easily, throwing temper tantrums, arguing, lying and cheating, using vulgar language, being secretive or passive, being abusive and hostile, and similar unpleasant behaviors. They may have learned habits of not responding when spoken to, not being on time, or being constant complainers. It is important to understand that the process of modeling is usually one of the roots of antisocial and amoral behavior in young children. But it can be a positive force as well. We need to help and encourage our children to learn new modes of behavior without punishing them for behaving the way they have seen us (or siblings) behave. At the same time, we need to start changing some of our own behaviors, because that is the most logical way to help effect change in others. It is not easy for parents to change lifelong habits, but when you see the changes you make reflected in your children's new behavior, it becomes worth the effort.

Rhythm

Each of us is rhythmically unique. From birth on, some people naturally move slowly; some move fast. Some need more sleep while some need less. Some are quick, alert, and full of energy; some are more lethargic and easygoing. When children are forced into rhythms that go against their own natural paces, they are placed under a great deal of stress that frequently results in negative behavior. It is important that you watch carefully and get to know which of your children are early-in-the-day persons and which do better when allowed time to move more slowly until they get started. Gradually, even though their basic natural rhythms do not change, children adjust to the routines of those with whom they spend most of their time. In fact, with a little care and concern, schedules for the entire family can be planned to draw out the best that each family member has to offer.

Physical discomfort or illness

Children's physical condition has a direct relationship to their behavior. Hunger, fatigue, or the onset of illness can cause your children to be short-tempered or easily upset. When a normally well-behaved child demonstrates unusual behavior, check for headache, fever, earache, or stomachache. Children who appear listless or unusually irritable should be encouraged to rest and stay home from school. Red or watery eyes (with or without a runny nose) should be cause for concern. Even if the symptoms are due to an allergy rather than a pending cold or flu, they make children feel uncomfortable and thus may cause a change in behavior. Chronic, subtle illnesses may cause cooperative children to develop negative patterns of behavior. It is important that you be alert to changes in your children's actions and seek professional medical help when it is warranted.

Reinforcement

Parents often unwittingly reinforce misbehavior by overreacting to it. By overreacting, I mean expressing extreme emotional reactions—shouting, threatening, coercing, nagging, spanking, or using other physical punishment. It has been shown time and again that children who are frequently punished for negative behavior require more and more frequent punishment. They become conditioned to the idea that misbehavior is expected of them and that it gets attention. Angry, confused, or lonely children will repeat offenses in order to control or get attention from their parents and others. If it works, they will continue to repeat the behavior. Recognizing a pattern of reinforcement can be the first step toward instituting alternatives to punitive discipline that will help children learn positive behavior patterns without reinforcing the negative ones.

Too many *no*'s

How many times do you say *no* or *don't* or *not now* to your children during the course of a day? Children need to be given firm limits, and they need to be reminded if what they are doing, planning, or saying is inappropriate in regard to social mores, safety, or family rules. But too many *no*'s will negate our best intentions and make children feel harangued and inhibited.

The process of growth and development takes many years and is best accomplished through trial and error under the gentle guidance of parents and other care-givers. Our role is to help our children develop the skills to make appropriate decisions. We not only need to give them many opportunities to experience the consequences of their own actions, but we must also protect them and others by giving clear, explicit reasons for the *no*'s that we give them. Many abrupt *no*'s can be avoided by the use of alternatives that consider your children's feelings, your feelings, and the traditional parent-child power struggle. Here are some examples:

Hasty Response	Considered Response
No, you can't taste that. We're going to eat soon.	I know it smells good. Here's a little taste. How is it?
No, you can't play soccer today.	I know you would like to play soccer. But after that nosebleed, it would be better for you to do something that's less active.

Hasty Response	Considered Response
No, your brother is reading that book.	When Larry is through with it, you may have it.
No, you can't have any more.	That was good fruit salad. I have to remember to make more next time.
Don't touch that.	You may look at that plant, but touching hurts it.
No. It's too high.	That looks high to me. I'll stand close and watch while you try it out.
No, that's not in the recipe.	Why don't you put just a little in this separate cup and see whether it's a good idea or not.
No, it's too sharp.	Let's see how sharp that knife is. It seems too sharp. I think you need to wait until I have time to help you.

It is important for your children to learn that the difference between *no* and *yes* is a matter of careful consideration, not a hasty response. If they observe how carefully you weigh the pros and cons of a situation, they will learn to do so too.

Masked or manipulative behavior

Among the most difficult situations to handle are those in which children mask a feeling or need—usually by behaving inappropriately. Children don't usually know they are "coding" their behavior; they are simply using a defense mechanism they have developed in response to basic insecurities in their relationships with others. For example, take a child who has broken some object and provokes punishment by starting a fight with another child rather than by admitting the accident. Such a child may be feeling anxiety and guilt, which are too difficult for the child to cope with. Hitting someone else may be an easy way to release those feelings. Another example is a child who is domineering to the point of alienating siblings and playmates. The child really wants friends, but because of a very poor self-image, he or she needs to be in control of all situations. Such children lack trust and need much help in working out hidden insecurities.

Punishment is not what these children need, although that is what they usually get. They need to have you talk with them, listen to them, and give them feedback. They need to have their self-confidence built up, one small step at a time, until they can cope with flexibility. They need to experience honesty and kept promises in order to kindle or rekindle their own feelings of trust.

Children who have manipulative behavior benefit from make-believe games. Through these games, usually called dramatic play, these children can role-play the people they know and act out the things they don't understand or the things that worry them. Eventually dramatic play helps them work out their misperceptions of the world about them. With support and encouragement from caring parents, they may eventually be able to overcome their need to try to manipulate others by their behavior.

Testing limits

Children go through developmental stages in which testing the limits of their own control is very important. A constant theme in childhood is children's need to feel in control of their lives as much as possible. Testing limits is one of the ways they try out that control: with trepidation, children begin to try out ideas they get, watching you to see if you will approve—and how far they can go if you disapprove. This helps them to build their feelings of autonomy and independence. On the other hand, insecure children may deliberately try to do something they know you disapprove of to test whether you really care. Children are often comforted to know that a parent will help them control their actions and their emotions when they themselves are unable to be in control.

Personality conflicts

Personality conflicts are not something that a parent will admit to openly. Nonetheless there are, unfortunately, situations where the personality of a parent's own child may be distasteful to that parent. Clashes will occur frequently between a parent and child whose personalities conflict. It is the parent's responsibility to recognize personality clashes and, little by little, try to break through the irrational barriers. In the meantime, the parent must take extra precaution not to let the child become a scapegoat for everything that goes wrong. Often, a parent's unspoken rejection of the child causes rebellious behavior in that child. Ironically, the conflict often involves the child whose personality most resembles that of the parent. Perhaps the parent sees in the child a reflection of those qualities that he or she has never liked.

These feelings are normal, and you shouldn't feel guilty about them. But such feelings should be acknowledged. Personality conflicts should be overcome for the benefit of the child involved. Acknowledging the feeling behind such conflicts is the first step in overcoming the problem.

Extreme Cases

As you read this book, you may say to yourself, "That may be OK for most children, but she doesn't know Diana," or "I'd like to see her try to work some of those tricks with Manuel," or "Well, she doesn't know my kids." Perhaps you may think, "She must know all nicely behaved children," or even, "She made it all up. She's living in a dream world. She should meet some real kids."

This book is about real kids. I have worked for many years with normal children who bite, kick, push, fight, yell, swear, break things, throw things, knock things down, talk back, insult others, lie, steal, tease, and do all of the other things that children are subject to doing and that get them into trouble with others.

As a teacher and school director, I've been so badly bitten by a two-year-old that I needed medical attention, and I've been called unprintable names by a four-year-old. I've had money stolen from my purse by a six-year-old and had my face slapped by an eight-year-old. I've gotten very angry and frustrated and full of despair, just as you have many times, as a parent. I've been discouraged, embarrassed, and made to feel like a fool. But I've never knowingly rejected a child, and I've seldom deliberately punished a child. I've spent hour upon hour alone with children, helping them to sort out their feelings and studying them to find causes for their lack of behavioral control.

Hostile children

Uncooperative, hostile, belligerent children may need to have professional guidance. They usually have known impatience, coercion, threats, reprisals, and punishments. They have been berated and they are confused. The treatment they have received has modeled ways to coerce, threaten, punish, and berate others. These children develop such poor self-images that they can only function in ways that help them live up to those images. They are literally starved for affection; they don't let anyone get close to them because they don't feel close to anyone. They are lonely and full of despair, even if they live within large families. They feel so hated that they spend much of their time building fantasy worlds and retaliating with hate toward others. In most cases, their uncooperativeness will have been reinforced by the very discipline imposed on them for that behavior.

These children need help in learning that it is only their behavior that is rejected, not themselves. You need to find ways to express new expectations and practice new ways of interrelating positively. Problem solving to change the behavior of belligerent children requires careful planning, cooperation of the entire family, persistence, cooperation with the school the children attend, and, most of all, patience.

In approaching each child's needs, three steps should be taken: (1) search out the cause of the behavior; (2) develop a consistent plan for helping the child learn new modes of behavior; and (3) find new ways to interrelate with one another. Compare the following examples of communication between a parent and child:

Belligerent Pattern of Interaction

Good morning, darling, time to get up. Time to get up, I said. If you don't get up I'll come in there and do it for you. Damn it, I said get up right now.

Did you brush your teeth? Are you sure you're telling me the truth?

Not that shirt. It's filthy. If you had put it in the hamper like I told you to, it wouldn't be lying around for you to put on. No! Don't you have any brains? Not that shirt! It's cold out today. Don't argue with me. Wear this warm shirt. Boy, you sure know how to get someone in a bad mood in the morning. All you think about is yourself.

Cooperative Pattern of Interaction

Good morning, darling. Time to get up and get dressed. Here are the clothes we got ready last night. Call me if you need help. We can eat breakfast as soon as you've brushed your teeth.

I'm glad I have this chance to sit and eat breakfast with you because I won't see you again until dinnertime. Tonight after dinner we can read that new rocket book.

By adopting a nonpunitive, humane approach, you can bring about a change in the behavior of hostile, belligerent children. You can improve the behavior of sarcastic, sassy, arrogant children, or children who are noisy and overactive or who are sullen and morose. It may take a great deal of trial and error before you find the methods that work best with your children. You can restructure your approach by following these four steps:

1. Give them an accepting, consistent, caring environment. Consistency is very important. In addition to enduring the normal tensions of family living, your children may feel that they are faced with ongoing inconsistencies and rejection when communicating with you. They may feel unloved and unwanted.

2. Use the "magic list" of Nondiscipline Discipline in Part II of this book. The list suggests alternatives to punitive discipline; it is like magic, and it will work. Choose the alternatives that are most appropriate for you and your children. Be patient, remembering always that your goals are to promote growth and learning and to help your children learn more acceptable ways of responding and interacting. You need to help build their self-esteem and help them experience and recognize acceptance.

3. Get to know your children's teachers, establishing lines of communication that will help you keep each teacher informed of your efforts, your successes, and your failures. Show the teacher the magic list and try to get it introduced into your children's school. Working together with the teachers can be one of the most positive steps you will take.

4. Begin problem solving. As previously stated, every inappropriate behavior has a cause, just as every appropriate behavior has a cause. Everything we do, we do because we want something. We have to find out what our children's real wants are and then find ways of supplying those wants if they are appropriate. Or we must change them if they are inappropriate.

Emergencies

There are emergency situations in which drastic action must be taken because of extremely irrational or violent behavior on the part of one of your children. Emergencies are not part of the growth-learning process. They are not punishment. They are simply emergencies.

When someone's health or safety is at risk, you must take immediate action and do whatever is necessary to avert disaster. For example, if three-year-old Tommy is ready to clobber his little sister Janie on the back of the head with a ten-inch metal truck, grab the truck out of Tommy's hands. If you're too far away, shout "Tommy!" long enough to distract him. Then say, "Put that truck down right now!" very firmly and positively, leaving no doubt in Tommy's mind that he must really put it down. Simultaneously, you should be moving toward him to physically enforce your order if Tommy doesn't respond. Meanwhile, you will have interrupted his action long enough to keep him from hurting Janie.

Don't stop to worry about what a more experienced parent would do, or whether or not you have decided to do the right thing. The important thing is to take immediate action and do whatever is necessary to avert disaster. If you need to yell, scream, grab, pull—whatever is most expedient to save the situation—do so. You will have plenty of time afterward to evaluate your actions and decide whether or not it was appropriate. You can discuss it with others and decide what type of action might have been more appropriate. You may even discuss it with your children, after the excitement has subsided, and get some positive reactions from them. Just remember that whatever methods of discipline you usually use, a more drastic approach during an emergency will not ruin a good approach, nor will it scar your child for life.

Running away from home

There are occasions when children become so angry that they decide to run away from home. When children see that no one is coming after them, they usually will turn around and return of their own accord. However, even though ignoring a would-be runaway may be the best course to take, it may not be safe. You must judge for yourself whether your child would be in danger if allowed the freedom to leave. It depends on your neighborhood, the traffic, the people you know in the neighborhood, the personality of your child, and whether or not this is the first time your child has "left."

Helpful hints

When children become so emotionally overwrought that you need to take drastic action to help them regain control of themselves, the following are some methods which have been used successfully at one time or another in extreme cases of difficult behavior:

1. Put your arms around your child from the rear and hug tight until calm is restored.

2. Remove a screaming, arm-flailing child from the rest of the family by standing to the side of the child and picking him or her up from around the waist. Hold the child at a 45-degree angle, head down, with the legs reaching over one of your shoulders. You can carry even a heavy child in this position without being hit or kicked and thus remove the child from an "audience" without a fight. The lifting and carrying should be done firmly but gently; there should be no hint of punishment in it. It is not demeaning; but the child is helpless. I have never used this carrying method on a child more than once. No matter how out-of-control the behavior seems to be, if I reach for the waist as I've done before, the child will usually say, "I'll come by myself." Merely saying this helps the child to regain control over seemingly uncontrollable actions. Remember, though, I am suggesting it only if you are in danger of being hurt or if the child is uncontrollable.

3. Belligerent, withdrawn, or hyperactive children often avoid looking you in the eyes. There have been times when I've been able to regain such a child's attention by having someone else hold the child's head gently but firmly so that it can't be moved from side to side. At the same time, I will hold the child gently by the arms and look directly into his or her eyes, saying, "It's all right. I know you're very angry. You can talk about it. First, I need you to sit down right here so I know where you are," or something appropriate to the situation. Talking to the child while looking directly in the eyes usually establishes a communication that enables me to use a restorative approach such as humor, discussion, helping the child to

express feelings in a legitimate manner, or some other approach I feel will help meet the child's—and my— immediate needs.

Not all children demonstrate such bizarre behavior that you need to take the extreme measures described above. But knowing how to deal humanely with extreme cases of difficult behavior will help with those everyday behavior problems that call for less drastic action. In the following section of this book (Part II), we will examine the many ways to deal with your children humanely in your everyday interactions with them.

Part II
The Magic List:
Alternatives to Punitive Discipline

CHAPTER FIVE

Disciplinary Attitudes: An Introduction to Nondiscipline Discipline

Parents can waste a great deal of energy engaging in conflict with their children under the guise of discipline. Indeed, traditional methods of discipline too often fail us because they are not very effective. Children need guidance—that is an accepted fact. They need help developing skills to make wise decisions for themselves. They need protection for their health and safety. They need some limits, directions, and rules to follow. But discipline should be geared to the development of self-respect, healthy interpersonal relationships, and problem-solving skills. Parents should consider discipline methods that will lessen, rather than increase, pointless conflict. This may require a change in basic attitudes about discipline. My program of Nondiscipline Discipline, which offers alternatives to punitive, abusive, and irrational control of children, exemplifies such a change.

Traditional Disciplinary Attitudes

Unfortunately, many of our child-rearing traditions are based on negative attitudes. Parents sometimes feel more responsible for preventing their children from doing wrong than for helping the children do right. Such a negative approach fosters negative control techniques: threats, disapproval, and punishment to create guilt, fear, and submission. For years, it has been taken for granted that, because a

75

child "belonged" to a parent, the parent had the right to physically abuse the child. We didn't say "abuse," however; we said "spank." But it is abuse. When discipline methods involve force and verbal and physical hurting, it is abuse. Children, as a result, suffer shame and humiliation.

The following are categories and examples of punishment common in households today. As you read them, think of whether you have used any of them. Consider whether they have contributed to harmony and cooperation between you and your children, and try to identify the underlying attitudes they express.

- Childish control: "You're a bad boy." "No, no, no." "If you bite him again, I'll bite you."

- Punitive control: "Just for that, no television for you all week." "You can spend the rest of the day in your room." "Write 'I will listen to my father' one hundred times." This category also includes ignoring or isolating children, locking them in closets, and withholding meals.

- Abusive verbal control: "Why can't you hurry up? What a slowpoke! I've told you twenty times now to hurry, hurry!" "What's wrong? Are you too stupid to figure out how to do it?" "Now none of us can watch TV—all because of you. You make me sick!" This also includes nagging and nit-picking.

- Abusive physical control: This includes spanking; biting back; slapping; poking; pinching; tightly gripping the shoulder, neck, arm, face, or other parts of the child's body; pulling the child by the hair or ear; pushing the child; knocking the child down; rapping the child's knuckles; or hitting the child with any object.

- Irrational control: This includes any combination of the other types of control, accompanied or characterized by intense anger, harangues, fierce expressions, or threatening gestures.

In the long run, harsh discipline usually doesn't work. Children who are spanked, for example, are spanked over and over again. What we are really teaching them by such punitive methods is that violence, abuse, and humiliation of others is acceptable behavior, as long as you are bigger than the person being disciplined. It's not only the children who suffer. Parents, too, suffer shame and humiliation when they find themselves losing control and shouting at their children and punishing them repeatedly. Parents' self-esteem suffers and they lose confidence in their parenting skills. Everyone loses when parents waste time patrolling and punishing their children. Punishment seldom fosters harmony and cooperation between family members. In fact, it usually creates a very negative home environment. The underlying attitude that punishment expresses is that children want to misbehave.

Nondiscipline Discipline Attitudes

As long as our system of discipline is based on the expectation that children want to misbehave, children will live up to that expectation; if we use discipline based on the attitude that children want to cooperate, they will live up to that expectation instead. Nondiscipline Discipline is actually a system of attitudes. It is based on friendly, caring approaches toward the health, development, and needs of our children. It gives careful regard to feelings and emotions, to unique differences between individuals, and to promoting an atmosphere of acceptance, tolerance, patience, and love.

Nondiscipline Discipline, with its rational, analytical approach, permits you to bring professionalism to your role as a parent. You no longer have to be a dictator or mock prison guard. It requires that you ask yourself, in each instance of a child's misbehavior, "How can I help my child find an alternative way of behaving without reinforcing the behavior I would like to see stopped, or changed?" The assumption— the attitude—underlying this kind of discipline is that it will help your children learn and grow in harmony with one another and with the entire family. There is also an assumption that if you want your children to change, you must be willing to change as well.

Setting clear rules and precise limits

A wholesome family setting in which Nondiscipline Discipline is practiced is one in which you, the parent, with the cooperation and knowledge of your children, have set explicit, understandable limits and rules for personal conduct. As you set out your basic guidelines, you may find that the following considerations will enhance the process:

- Include children in the rule-setting process to help them learn responsibility and discriminative thinking. Your children will adhere more closely to rules they have helped to establish and evaluate than ones which have been imposed on them arbitrarily.

- Be honest. Tell your children what behavior really bothers you, even if it is only an idiosyncrasy of yours. Let them tell you what you do that bothers them.

- Be realistic. Most rules should be founded logically on concerns for health, safety, care of property, and consideration for one another. The child's ability to use logic doesn't begin to develop until the elementary school years, and even then it takes time for children to become skilled in its use. So, cause-and-effect explanations of why certain rules are necessary must take into account the immature perceptions of preschool-age children. They should be worded as simply—and with as few words—as possible.

- Be democratic. Rules must be fair. They must apply equally to all. At the same time, they must be geared to the ages and developmental capabilities of your children. Thus, the same rule might be applied with variations, if age or ability requires it.

Soliciting cooperation

Once you have committed yourself to nondisciplinary attitudes, established clear rules and precise limits, and begun using good communication methods, you will be well on your way to treating your commitment to parenthood with professional finesse. You can begin to adopt the following principles for ensuring your children's cooperation with your own positive efforts:

- Be precise. When you make a request, make it clear to whom you are addressing your comments. Politely and firmly say what you want and when you want it. Assume that your children would rather cooperate than not.

- Be consistent. Make sure your requests are in keeping with the rules you have all established together.

- Be fair. Be sure the requests you make are fair and apply equally to all your children. Make sure you don't play favorites.

- Say something only once. Let your children know that, from now on, you expect a response the first time. Sometimes a child hears but doesn't listen. Be sure you get your children's attention first. Sometimes you might have to add, "I called you," or "I'm talking to you."

- Enforce your requests. You need to be assertive but at the same time remain kind, caring, and gentle. Following through with a request can mean guiding your child to some location by cupping your hand under the child's elbow or gently taking the child's hand. In an emergency, you may need to lift up your child bodily. If you do so, be kind, caring, and gentle.

- Don't argue. Be persistent but don't provoke a confrontation and don't allow your child to provoke one. It takes two to have an argument; simply refuse to argue. If you're unable to enforce what you have requested, it may be wise to walk away from it.

- Remain flexible. Sometimes you might say, "I can see you won't cooperate with me today. I'll ask you another time." "Another time" is better than "later" or "tomorrow" because it's less specific. When you use this technique, you'll find that your children sometimes will do what was asked—even though they may wait until you leave the scene.

The Magic List of Alternatives

Traditional methods of discipline and child-rearing are so ingrained that they are almost automatic responses. I have developed a "magic list" of alternatives to them. Each item on the list is an alternative to an item listed as a traditional punitive response. The magic list items are described in detail in the chapters that follow. Most parents have used these alternative methods at one time or another. Parents I know who have used my magic list during the last few years claim that these alternatives are very successful. Teachers who have used the list in nursery and elementary schools have found the list to be successful. After studying this list and trying some of the alternatives, you may have other items to add.

Traditional Punitive Response	The Magic List of Alternatives
React impulsively.	Anticipate trouble.
Issue sarcasm and threats.	Give gentle reminders.
Find fault and scold.	Distract to a positive model.
Be grouchy and irritable.	Inject humor.
Make rigid demands.	Offer choices.
Belittle or ignore.	Give praise or compliments.
Criticize and coerce.	Offer encouragement.
Make ambiguous comments.	Clarify messages.
Nit-pick or nag.	Overlook small annoyances.
React hastily and automatically.	Deliberately ignore provocations.
Be stubborn and unbending.	Reconsider the situation.
Punish.	Point out natural, or logical, consequences.
Impose isolation.	Provide renewal time.
Make authoritarian demands.	Give hugs and caring.
Humiliate, impose guilt, and punish.	Arrange discussion among the children.
Lecture.	Provide discussion with an adult.

Which alternative to choose

There is no simple answer as to which alternative to choose. Usually, any one of several alternatives can be selected for a particular incident. The important thing to remember is that *automatic* responses are self-defeating. Your children, being individuals with unique characteristics, personalities, and skills, deserve individual consideration. Each situation is likewise unique and must be evaluated to determine the degree and method of intervention that will produce the desired results. Just stopping to think about the situation, instead of responding on an emotional level, immediately raises your standing as a parent.

In the following example, several alternative responses are given as possibilities for the same situation:

Sarah and Jessica both want to play with the tape recorder. The conflict results in a quarrel between the sisters.

Typical Response	Alternative Response
I'm sick and tired of your quarreling and I don't intend to put up with it for one minute more.	**Give gentle reminders.** *Parent*: Girls, please share. or *Parent*: It needs to be quiet in here. I'm trying to read.
Parent: If you keep aggravating me like this, I don't know what I'm going to do with you two girls. Give me that tape recorder. I'll show you who's boss around here. Now, neither one of you can use it. Go to your rooms and stay there. I don't want to hear one word from either of you.	**Reconsider the situation.** *Parent*: One of you can use my recorder. I like the way you've been practicing your songs on it. or *Parent*: I'm sorry we have only one tape recorder. I know it makes it hard, but maybe someday we'll be able to get another one so you can each have your own. Meanwhile, you may want to share.
Parent: I don't know which one of you two is more selfish. Of course, if you knew how to share, I'd let you play with the recorder. But you don't know how to share. You know only how to argue.	**Arrange discussion among the children.** *Parent*: I don't know what you two are quarreling about, but I think you should stop arguing and discuss it quietly between yourselves.

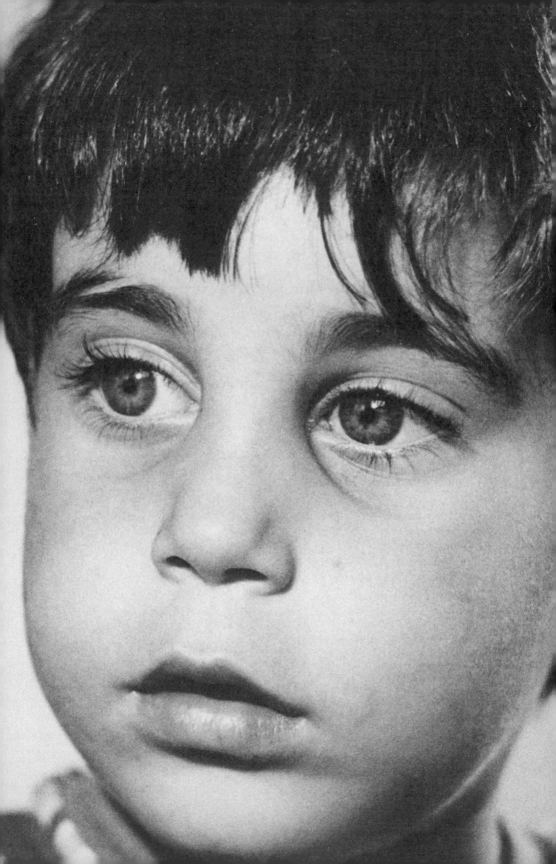

Typical Response	Alternative Response
Parent: Since you two can't seem to work things out between yourselves, I'll tell you what to do. Give me that tape recorder! You may not play with it for the next two weeks.	Offer choices. *Parent*: You'll have to decide whether you want to share the tape recorder, play with it individually according to a schedule we work out, or not play with it at all.
Parent: All you ever do is fight and argue. Can't you ever get along? Do you think I want to hear your silly bickering?	Overlook small annoyances. *Parent*: Will you two please close the door? It's too noisy.

The typical responses serve to blow a minor incident out of proportion. Instead of helping the children toward a different kind of behavior, they serve to humiliate the children, lower their self-esteem, inflict guilt, and increase their inner stress. The alternative responses model patience and self-control. They express an expectation that the children are responsible for their own behavior. And they give the children opportunities to work out a system of cooperative play. Any of the alternatives is a satisfactory response, since they each serve the purpose of helping the children find a way to solve their difficulties.

Of course, you won't use all the alternatives from the magic list at once. You'll learn to use them gradually when they seem comfortable and appropriate. To help you start using Nondiscipline Discipline in your home, follow these steps:

1. Read all of the alternatives from beginning to end. Put a paper clip on those pages you wish to reread for clarification or validity.

2. Try out one or two alternatives each day for one week. Try to enlist the cooperation of your spouse or any other adults living in your home. If there are teenagers in the home, tell them you need their help in following the magic list. It will probably result in better communication with them, too, since it's based on principles of humane communication.

3. As you concentrate on one alternative on a particular day, evaluate that alternative at the end of the day. Think about how comfortable you were with it and how effective it was for you.

4. Post the magic list at two or three places around the house. Refer to it quickly when you're in doubt about how to respond to a given situation. Except in an emergency, take the time to decide which alternative will be most effective.

5. Modify the magic list by adding your own ideas.

6. With children who have significant or chronic behavior problems, use the utmost patience while you look for probable causes and devise appropriate solutions to those problems.

The Magic List: Alternatives to Punitive Discipline

Use the magic list as a reminder of alternatives from which you can choose. It will help you in the ongoing development and refinement of your own nondisciplinary attitudes. Consciously choosing from the magic list of alternatives instead of resorting to the more typical, traditional reactions will open many new doors for you—doors to the joy of parenting and the wonders of childhood.

Anticipate trouble.

Give gentle reminders.

Distract to a positive model.

Inject humor.

Offer choices.

Give praise or compliments.

Offer encouragement.

Clarify messages.

Overlook small annoyances.

Deliberately ignore provocations.

Reconsider the situation.

Point out natural, or logical, consequences.

Provide renewal time.

Give hugs and caring.

Arrange discussion among the children.

Provide discussion with an adult.

CHAPTER SIX

Alternatives: Preventing Inappropriate Behavior

Prevention is often the best cure. This concept applies to behavior problems in the home as well as to other aspects of our life. The five "magic list" alternatives discussed in this chapter are particularly useful for nipping trouble in the bud.

Anticipate Trouble

Anticipating trouble is one of the most important alternatives; with it you can prevent trouble before it starts. Anticipating includes considering the ages and personalities of your children and being able to guess at their likely responses to various situations. Through anticipation, you can manipulate your family schedules and plan family activities that are appropriate for your children, thus motivating productive and positive behavior.

First, you can control the physical environment in the home to minimize stress and promote trust and cooperation. Anticipating also means being alert to the emotional environment. When unusual or stressful situations occur in the family, you can anticipate that the children will be affected. Make sure that you alleviate their fears and explain things in as simple terms as you can so that they will understand. Even if the events that take place are joyful, they still involve change and excitement. It will be hard for your children to be on their best behavior unless you make some kind of advance plans to help them adjust to and participate in the event. Sometimes the emotional variables are quite subtle and, therefore, less predictable. By being alert to your children's moods, you may recognize—by their actions and their body language—when they are troubled or confused. When a situation begins to deteriorate, intervene before trouble begins, in order to prevent a more serious confrontation.

The following are some examples of how anticipating trouble works:

David is playing in the family room. His mother comes into the room and asks him to come to dinner. As he rushes off toward the kitchen, she realizes David is leaving a big mess behind.

Typical Response	Anticipating Trouble
You get back here. You can't leave that stuff in such a big mess. Get that cleaned up right now. You should know that, without my telling you. You make me sick. (The feelings generated are embarrassment, belligerence, tension, and lowered self-esteem.)	It's almost dinnertime. In five minutes I want you to put those things away. You can take them out again after dinner if you want to. (Caring and understanding are expressed; helpfulness is encouraged.)

Mr. Taylor watches his children practice softball near the house.

Typical Response	Anticipating Trouble
When the ball smashes the window, Mr. Taylor says: That was a stupid thing to do. You should have known better than to play ball so close to the house. That's going to cost a lot of money to fix. I guess we'll just have to take it out of your allowance. There goes that trip to Disneyland. (A window is broken, and the children are made to feel stupid and guilty for what was just a matter of poor judgment. The trip to Disneyland shouldn't have any bearing on the replacement of the window.)	Before anything happens, Mr. Taylor says: You might accidentally break the window playing over there. You'd better play ball behind the garage. That's a much safer place. (Appropriate caution is modeled for the children; caring is expressed, while trouble is averted.)

It is three days before Thanksgiving, and a big dinner is planned. The house must be cleaned, food must be prepared, and there is great excitement throughout the house.

Typical Response

Hurry up now. Everybody has to help clean. Come on, come on. Don't be so slow. I don't want any fooling around, we just don't have time for that. You both had better toe the mark or you will spend your day being sorry. Here, take this and dust the furniture. Not both of you! How dumb can you be? You both act like you've never seen a clean house before. Get to work! (This parent is so keyed up that existing tension is heightened, and negative feelings will, no doubt, prevail for the rest of the day. The children surely will get into trouble, because they are being made to feel worthless.)

Anticipating Trouble

Let's sit down for a minute to decide what everyone's going to do. Allison, you can dust the furniture for me. And Paul can vacuum the rugs. If you do it right now, you'll be through just in time to watch television for half an hour before changing your clothes. I sure like it when you help me. (In anticipation of the children's heightened tension, this parent helps them plan their time. Planning is a productive, calming technique. Overall, stress is reduced for the children and the parent.)

The weather has been stormy for several days, and the children have had to play indoors, which puts a lot of pressure on the entire household. Both the children and their parents are irritable. But today is Saturday and the sun is shining brightly.

Typical Response

Well, what a nice day for a change. It's too bad you kids have been such brats, because otherwise I could let you go out and play. I think you'll just have to stay in and clean up your room. Maybe the next time it rains you'll remember how to behave. (Rather than helping the children regain their self-control and giving them a healthy opportunity to relieve some of their tension, this parent is only compounding the situation and encouraging further deterioration of the children's behavior.)

Anticipating Trouble

How lucky that the weather has finally cleared up enough so you can go outdoors to play! First let me hear you both agree not to fight. Then you can really enjoy the nice day and have a good time playing together. (This parent is anticipating that after being indoors all week, they might be overenthusiastic in their play. By having them commit themselves to some limits, the parent is encouraging responsibility and setting up a good day for everyone.)

The family is getting ready to move. They are doing some last-minute packing in preparation for the truck that will come the next day.

Typical Response

Parent: OK, Stevie, calm down now. I can see what kind of day we're going to have. Now, you'll just have to straighten yourself out. You know, you're not the only one who's ever moved. People do it every day. I've got too much work to do getting the rest of this stuff packed. Stay out of my hair. (Within five minutes, Stevie has taken out all of his toys that had been packed and has begun throwing them around the living room.)
Parent: I knew it. You had no right to get into that box. Now, pick up that junk and stay in your room. That will straighten you out. (This parent made no attempt to help Stevie cope with the trauma of moving. In addition, Stevie now feels guilty for being confused about having his toys packed up.)

Anticipating Trouble

Parent: Stevie, you're really excited about moving, aren't you? Here, let's take some time to talk about it. Let me rock you for a while and you can tell me how you feel.
Stevie: I like my house.
Parent: It is a nice house, isn't it? I like it too. I hope we'll like our new house just as much as we like this house.
Stevie: Don't go, please don't go.
Parent: I'm not going anyplace, except when we all go together to our new house. First, the big truck will come, and you can help the movers carry your toys to the truck. How's that?
Stevie: And I got big muscles, too.
Parent: Yes. Now, you can play with these toys I left out for you. I'm going to pack these glasses. We can talk while I'm doing it.
Stevie: I'm going to ride my trike. (Anticipating his worries, this parent puts Stevie at his ease. Reassured, Stevie's even able to go outside and play.)

Give Gentle Reminders

Gentle reminders are a helpful way to build trust and self-confidence in children. They are never sarcastic, demeaning, or embarrassing. When they are properly conveyed, gentle reminders also let children know they have someone on whom they can depend and to whom they can look for help in maintaining their self-control.

Using gerunds

A gerund is a noun created from a verb. It always ends with *"ing."* Gerunds can be used as gentle reminders and are especially effective with preschool children. They also work well in pressure situations with older children. I discovered the usefulness of gerunds as reminders quite accidentally. At one time in my career, I worked for a European-born psychologist. She frequently used gerunds in working with children. She not only had an innate ability to understand children and to create harmonious experiences for them, but she never had to say anything to them twice. Later, I found myself frequently using her manner of talking to children. The children responded much more consistently when I used that method than when I spoke to them in my normal manner.

When I analyzed this curious fact, I realized that if I say to a child, "We don't run in the house," the child may think, "You don't but I do. In fact, I'm doing it now." If I say, "Don't run in the house," the child may think, "Later, I won't run in the house, even though I am doing it now." But if I say, "Walking!" the child will slow down immediately. The gerund has the same connotation as the command "Stop running right now." Gerunds give you a method of seeking responses from children by using the shortest, simplest, gentlest type of reminder. You can use them in virtually every situation.

Typical Response	Using Gerunds as Reminders
Please sit down and wait.	Waiting.
You need to help your sister pick up the blocks.	Helping.
Jennie, please don't bother your brother. He doesn't like that.	Leaving him alone.
Watch out how you're carrying that. You'll spill it.	Not spilling. or Being careful.
Keep your fingers out of those cupcakes. That's for the party.	Not touching.
Don't just leave it there on the floor. Pick it up.	Picking it up.

Typical Response	Using Gerunds as Reminders
This is a quiet time. You're supposed to be taking a nap, or at least resting. Be quiet now.	Resting.
I need to explain what I want you to do while I'm taking my shower. Please be quiet and listen.	Listening.
It doesn't look to me like you're doing your homework. You really can't be trusted, can you. I have to stay on top of you just as if you were a baby.	Studying.

The advantage of these and similar short phrases is that children seem to interpret them as really meaning "right now." When said with assertiveness, they will be responded to easily; I think children appreciate the lack of lengthy tirades and explanations.

My very favorite gerund reminder is "playing nicely." When you see cooperative behavior between two or more children beginning to deteriorate, approach them and say, casually but definitely, "Playing nicely." No nagging or lecturing. Just the two words. Then walk away. It says to your children, "I know you are capable of playing nicely and remembering the rules. I'll just give you a little reminder that will make the remembering easier for you." Time and again I have seen children stop what they were doing, think for a moment, and then resume their activity with less belligerence or moodiness.

The effectiveness of gerunds will be evident when you start hearing your children use them with one another. And don't be surprised if one day, when you have fallen into the trap of nagging or lecturing and not giving your children a chance to explain, they will say to you, "Mother, listening," or "Waiting, Father. Let me explain."

Some people have expressed concern that the use of gerunds as gentle reminders will result in their children growing up using incorrect language. I can only say I have used them with hundreds of children who have become excellent academic students. The use of gerunds as gentle reminders does not carry over into their regular use of language; just as their parents do, however, children may call forth a phrase or two that suits their purposes when they need instant response.

This technique is especially useful with older children who have been consistently hard to handle. Children who are seven, eight, or nine years old and have frequent problems of misbehavior may be surprised into cooperation by the use of gerund reminders. When your child is poised to run outdoors while you give some instructions, say, "Waiting." When your children are quarreling and letting their emotions get out of control, say "Discussing." When your child walks up to a playmate with clenched fists, ready to start a fight, say, "Touching softly." When some household excitement causes your child to start shouting out a string of crude remarks, say, "Talking nicely." When two children are quarreling over the possession of a toy, say, "Sharing." When your child says he'll finish mowing the lawn later, say, "Finishing now." When your child lies down on the sofa and starts to put his feet up on it, say, "Remembering." And to the parents reading this book: "Trying it." (Caution: Do not use this technique with your spouse.)

Nonverbal reminders

Not all gentle reminders need to be spoken. Some of the most effective reminders are nonverbal. For example:

- Nodding your head

- Catching a child's eye from across the room

- Smiling as you gently shake your head

- Touching gently on the shoulder or arm

- Holding your index finger up while cocking your head slightly toward the finger

Avoid looking or sounding angry and threatening if you want to give children gentle reminders. Such conduct may remind children of the rules but may also encourage defiance, since the message is that you really don't trust or respect them. Your facial expression is very important. Think of your own response to people whose expressions are pleasant when they ask something of you as compared with people who look angry or hostile. If you want your children to smile with ease, be sure that you smile for them.

Distract to a Positive Model

This is yet another type of reminder. It can be very effective if you have several children in the family, but it must be used sparingly. You have probably become aware that sometimes, when you scold one child, a younger child will start crying. By the same token, you can compliment a child for positive behavior, and a younger child might copy that behavior in an effort to receive a similar compliment.

When you use this technique, you need to take care not to let the positive comment about one child sound as if it were meant to humiliate, criticize, or deride another. The following examples show how this approach can be used much like a gentle reminder or to help children choose appropriate behavior.

Laura and Julie, ages five and six, are getting ready for bed.

Typical Response	Distracting to a Positive Model
Mother: Laura, you get those clothes up off the floor this minute. I don't know how you expect to have anything that looks decent, since you throw your things around. I shouldn't even get you anything nice. (This mother has humiliated her daughter, and she hasn't said anything to encourage the daughter to change her habits.)	*Mother*: Julie, I sure feel happy when I see how you put your clothes so neatly on the chair when you get undressed. (Laura immediately picks up her clothes from where she had left them on the floor. The mother was careful to use an "I" message, so Laura was not humiliated in any way.)

Jack and Paul, ages three and four, lie down for an afternoon nap. Jack is having trouble quieting down.

Typical Response	Distracting to a Positive Model
Mother: I told you to close your eyes and go to sleep. Don't you know that it's nap time? What's wrong with you today? I don't have time to keep coming in here to see if you're asleep. I have lots of work to do. Quiet down now. (pause) Why are you crying? Why can't you be like your brother? Look how nicely he's resting.	*Mother*: Paul, I like the way you're being so quiet. You really know how to get ready for your nap. (Jack looks at Paul and readjusts his position in bed.) *Jack*: Look, Mama, I go sleep too. *Mother*: And I like the way you're going to be quiet now, too.

Inject Humor

Humor is one of our greatest natural resources and should be used often with children. In appreciating the seriousness of their responsibilities, and burdened by the weight of their personal, business, and family problems, parents too often neglect this important aspect of communication. Children flourish when there is laughter, joy, and lighthearted repartee in their daily lives.

Very young children respond well to just plain silliness and will generally be more cooperative when humor is used. As children develop, they begin to appreciate jokes and riddles and continue to respond to silliness. They often get carried away with mimicry and clowning and let it overwhelm their original good intentions just to get some laughs going. Use care to balance humor with normal methods of communication.

In times of crisis or trouble, a note of humor can often interrupt a deteriorating situation and disrupt a pattern of growing tension. Laughter helps relieve tension and promotes a spirit of camaraderie. In times of solemnity and seriousness, some gentle humor can offset anxiety and increase children's ability to be cooperative.

In order to use humor and evoke joy, you first need to project a cheerful attitude. This is often very hard to do when you're tired, pressed for time, or worried. You can display cheerfulness by being enthusiastic and optimistic. Try to let your children know, not only by what you say but by your demeanor and your movements, that you are happy to be with them, despite what other problems you may have.

In using humor, avoid sarcasm. Never belittle anyone, but learn to laugh at yourself and have your children laugh with you. When you learn to laugh at yourself, you are declaring healthy "ownership" of imperfect behavior. Any time you can declare such ownership, it frees your children to feel comfortable in admitting their own imperfections and even to try to change their own behavior. As in all interactions with our children, the way we handle and use humor models for them ways they can handle and use it. Most important is remembering to laugh *with* your children, never *at* them.

Consider individual personalities

When using humor, take into account the differences in your children's personalities. If you have a child who is solemn and serious by nature, humor must be introduced gradually and with great gentleness. Such children may respond better to riddles than to outright jokes or kidding.

If your home suffers economic and emotional problems, it may be more difficult to generate humor. You can't force humor, but family members can encourage each other to smile, laugh, and appreciate the funny side of things. When you smile, your children will start doing so, too. They should be praised for even the slightest hint of a smile.

I like to make smile mirrors for children. It permits privacy while allowing children to explore their own facial expressions. The following are steps for making and using a smile mirror:

1. Glue a small pocket mirror in the center of a 9 × 12-inch piece of cardboard. (The cardboard can be a different size if you prefer.)

2. Have your children help you cut out pictures of smiling faces from magazines.

3. Have your children help you paste the pictures onto the cardboard surrounding the mirror. Rubber cement is a good adhesive to use, since you might want to move some of the faces around as the smile mirror develops.

4. When appropriate, suggest that a child go get the smile mirror and see how he or she is doing. You may want to help each child in the family make a smile mirror. Use the smile mirror yourself, too.

Lighthearted phrases

Not everyone is able to deliver humor with ease, especially when they're tired and pressed for time. If you aren't natural and comfortable with jokes and witty repartee, leave them to others—you can't fake things with children. You may be more at ease, however, injecting humor into everyday situations through the use of lighthearted phrases, as in the following examples:

Typical Response	Lighthearted Response
Everything seems to be going wrong.	Well, look at me, will you? It's my upside-down day.
No. It's easy to see that's not the way it goes.	Oh, oh. We goofed that time.
Oh, I'm sorry. That's not what I really meant to say. Excuse me. What I really meant was . . .	Oops! I must be silly. I think I said what I didn't mean.
Now, you just straighten up and listen to me. After all, I'm the one who's boss in this house and it's about time you understood that.	Hey! Wait a minute. I'm the parent around here—I think.
Oh, I forgot all about that. Well, it's too late now. I'll try to remember tomorrow.	Sometimes I think I didn't get up this morning, because I keep forgetting things. Here, touch me to see if I'm here.
How dare you laugh at me. Can't you show any respect for your father?	What's so funny? Oh, my shirt is hanging out in the back. I must look silly.
By golly, I'm sick and tired of wet towels all over the bathroom floor. Who left those towels in there? You'd better get in and pick them up right now, or I'll have to know the reason why.	Some brownies left some towels on the bathroom floor. But those brownies are gone now. Why don't you pretend you're a brownie and go pick up the towels?

After all, there's enough seriousness and tragedy in the world. Some gentle humor and lightheartedness can go a long way to help us all through normally stress-filled days.

Controlled, caring humor

Very young children have simple levels of humor. They respond to silliness, mimicry, clowning, and other kinds of actions. Great care must be taken not to let such humor be mistaken for ridicule or to deteriorate into chaos. On the contrary, controlled, caring humor can be a very productive means of distracting children from negative situations.

Jason, age four, reaches for a glass of milk on the table. The glass is too big for his small hands to hold, and he spills it.

Typical Response	Injecting Humor
Parent: Jason, when are you going to learn to keep your hands to yourself? Next time you want your milk, ask me for it. I should put your food on a tray; that way, you can go around spilling things all you want. I don't know why you don't grow up.	*Parent*: Oh, Jason, not again! I think you ought to be a big sponge so you could wipe up the things you spill. Here, honey. Here's a real sponge for you to use. *Jason*: Ho! Ho! I'm a big sponge.

Susan is doing her homework—some difficult subtraction problems. Her brother Paul comes running into the house and accidentally jiggles the table as he passes it. Susan screams, "Now see what you made me do?"

Typical Response	Injecting Humor
Parent (to Paul): Damn it! How many times have I told you not to run in this house? Don't you have any respect for anyone? You'd better go over and apologize to your sister. She has rights too, you know. Boy, you just don't think of anyone but yourself. *Paul*: I didn't do anything. You think she's so perfect. (He runs to his room and slams the door.)	*Parent*: Well, it looks like we have a cyclone loose today. Paul, I think your sister needs an apology. *Paul*: I'm sorry. I guess I was going too fast. *Susan*: Accepted. (She stops crying and goes back to work.)

Lily, age three, slipped on some water and went scooting across the floor on her bottom. When she came to a stop, she bumped the back of her head on the floor. Lily's parent began to laugh, knowing that she wasn't really hurt.

Typical Response

Parent: Oh, poor Lily. I'm sorry I'm laughing, but you looked so funny! (Lily cries loudly, of course, her injury compounded by what she interprets as ridicule.)

Injecting Humor

Parent: Oh, my goodness. The floor must have moved. Hey, floor! Stay still! Don't go around hitting people. (Lily, who had started to cry, is distracted long enough for her parent to give appropriate aid and comfort without having to cope with a tantrum. In a minute, Lily is off playing with her dolls.)
Lily (five minutes later, laughing): The floor hit me. Silly floor! (She waits for her parent to laugh with her and then goes back to playing.)

Offer Choices

When you give your children choices, you give them opportunities to be in control of a portion of their lives. This satisfies a basic need that we all have to be in control, and it can lead to greater cooperation in situations where you can't give choices. In addition to the satisfaction children derive from determining a portion of their lives, they are at the same time learning to make decisions in their adult lives.

We are all involved in a continuous process of decision-making as we pursue our daily lives. The more opportunities we have to make our own decisions, the greater our personal freedom. Children need guidance to deal with the ongoing problem of making choices. They need help learning to discriminate between good and bad choices and about the possible consequences of available choices. They need help in learning what is right and what is wrong, what is wise and what is unwise, what is appropriate and what is not, what is safe and what is unsafe. Children need to learn that they will eventually be able to make judgments and decisions on their own.

In giving them such experiences, it is wrong to punish your children when they make errors in judgment. Rather, you need to look at your own methods of decision-making and reevaluate how you are modeling the making of choices.

Be sure the choices you offer are all acceptable to you

The essential element in giving children choices is to be sure that all the choices you offer are acceptable to you. This is especially important in Nondiscipline Discipline. Choices must be offered with sincerity and honesty. Care must be taken that they are really choices and not threats. The following are examples of the difference between making threats and offering choices:

Typical "Threats"	Offering Choices
You either pick up those toys or stay in your room all day without eating.	Come over here and get a big hug; then you can pick up your toys; you can pick them up without a hug, or you can pick them all up first and get a big hug afterward.
If you don't put on your sweater, you can't go out today.	You can put on your sweater and I'll button it; or I can put it on you and you can button it; or if you like, I can put it on you and button it, too.
If you keep bumping your bike into the garage door, I'm going to take it away from you and not let you ride it for a long time.	You may put your bike away and play with something else; or you may ride it carefully along the sidewalk; or I can mark off a space on the driveway away from the garage door, for you to ride in. Which do you want to choose?
Stop grabbing those cars from your brother or I won't let you play at all.	You can give your brother half of the cars to play with, or you can play a game together with all of the cars, or I can divide them up for you. You can choose one of those ideas.
If I ever see you throwing things in the house, you'll have to stay inside all week.	You may stop throwing things right now and play with your puzzles; or you may read a book; or you may play quietly with this ball, rolling it on the floor to the wall.
If I ever catch you scribbling on the wall again, I'll take your crayons away from you and you won't ever have any in this house.	I feel bad when I see scribbling all over the wall, because it makes the house look ugly. You may scribble on this paper, or you may scribble on this pile of newspapers, or you can draw pictures on some paper plates.

Many times we make arbitrary statements that seem to us like choices. Really, they may either give no choice or they may make children feel ashamed or inadequate. Here are some examples:

Arbitrary Statements	Offering Choices
Here's a book to read while we're waiting.	Which of these books would you like to read while we're waiting?
Stop crying. Big boys don't cry.	It's OK to cry if you're feeling bad. Do you want to cry on this chair, on my lap, or in your room? or Do you want to cry loudly, softly, or not very much?
I can't work on my taxes if you're going to be so noisy.	You may go play in your room or stay in here and play very quietly or just read some books, because that's quiet, too.

Just as important as giving choices is recognizing that making choices is a skill to be learned. Very young children are often unable to decide things. When faced with several options, they will become confused unless you help them to make choices.

A training program for decision-making

You should start training your children immediately for decision-making. At first, give them choices about the everyday things that they will do anyway. Gradually, you can give more and more choices that will guide their behavior. Make a list of different kinds of choices to offer, such as:

- What color shirt to wear to school

- Which of three dresses to wear

- Whether to drink milk before breakfast, during breakfast, or afterward

- Whether to hear a bedtime story before getting into pajamas, after getting into them but not in bed, or after getting into bed

- Which story to read

- Whether to color, play with dolls, or play with a pegboard

- Whether to have an apple, a banana, or an orange

- Whether to go to the store with Daddy, help Mommy in the garden, or ride the new trike

- Whether to brush teeth before getting dressed or after getting dressed

- Whether to have a sandwich cut in half, in quarters, or not at all

Giving three choices

When you stop to analyze it, you may be amazed to realize that you have literally been telling your children every single thing to do, allowing no room for decision-making. Whenever possible in giving choices, try to give your children three things from which to choose. One choice may be easily discounted while the other two may pose a dilemma. If you offer only two possibilities, both of which are acceptable, it's really hard for a child to make a decision or to weigh one against the other. With three choices, however, there is more room for thinking about consequences.

Gradually increase the complexity of the choices you offer, but never ridicule your children when they have difficulty making decisions. Let them know that you don't want to decide for them. You can say, "Take your time," or "I can wait while you decide." Acknowledge that you realize it's sometimes very hard to choose. Then give praise when a choice has been made.

Another step in teaching decision-making is to give your children opportunities to select an array of choices. For example:

- I want you to help me plant a garden. Here are pictures of several kinds of flowers we could plant. This one is my favorite. Which other ones would you like to choose?

- We're going on a picnic with Grandma and Grandpa tomorrow. I'm going to make several kinds of sandwiches. What kinds do you think I should make?

Children will learn to arrive at and narrow down choices for the decision-making process. This can be a fun and creative way to exercise responsibility.

One good way to help develop decision-making skills is to make art and play materials available and be sure you give your children the freedom to use them in their own ways. Provide many different kinds and sizes of paper—thick, thin, large, small, round, rectangular, rough, smooth, colored, white, and so on. Just choosing which paper to use will call for making a decision. If their art supplies include crayons, chalks, charcoal, colored pencils, and moist watercolors, the children will get to choose which drawing and coloring tools to use. Having a variety of other art media—plasticine, moist modeling clay, textiles, and so on—available will offer even more choices. Art supplies and play materials should be stored in bright, colorful containers within your children's reach. This will encourage them to choose independently, without prompting from you.

Preschool children should have available many manipulative toys, blocks and boxes to build with, housekeeping toys such as dolls and stuffed animals and playhouse accessories, cars and trucks, and other playthings. Whatever their toys consist of, children should be encouraged to use them imaginatively and given praise when they do so.

Typical Response	Encouraging Choice
Why do you have to spread your things over the entire room? You could make the house just in this corner.	It looks like you've chosen to build our whole neighborhood today. I can even recognize which is our house.
You always make those same kinds of crooked buildings with those blocks. Why don't you make something that looks like a real house or a store or apartment building?	You decided to make those crooked buildings again, I see. I don't know how you do it. It seems very complicated to me.
That color really doesn't look good with red. Why don't you ask me? I could tell you all about which colors look good together. Then you could learn, too.	The colors you chose are kind of different from the ones I would use. But they sure balance one another. You're really learning to use your imagination in your pictures.

Typical Response	Encouraging Choice
That's not the way to use that. You're supposed to fit all those pieces into the different slots. Only the right ones fit, so you have to keep trying to figure it out. Now look, they all fell. I told you that wasn't what you're supposed to do with them.	I see you decided to stack those pieces in a big pile. That's hard. Oh, oh! I guess you went too fast. You'll just have to start over.

Notice that the words "choose" and "decide" are used often when presenting choices. Remember that these words help children realize they are involved in the decision-making process.

Adults frequently fall into the trap of thinking they are allowing children to make choices when, in fact, they themselves are making all the decisions. The following is a typical example:

> **Father** (on camping trip with rest of family): OK, everybody come here. Now that we've got the tent set up and everything is all laid out, it's time to do some planning. Now, first thing in the morning, we could go for a big hike to the top of that hill over there—unless, of course, you want to do something else.
>
> **Theresa:** I'm going fishing when I get up.
>
> **Manuel:** Not me; I'm going to hunt for rocks for my collection.
>
> **Father:** Those will be good things to do. But don't you think it's a good idea to go hiking first, before we get tired from doing other things? I love to go, especially right at dawn—just when the sun is coming up.
>
> **Mother:** I plan on sleeping late for a change.
>
> **Theresa:** But early in the morning is a good time to fish. It's so quiet and peaceful. I just can't wait.
>
> **Father:** It'll be quiet and peaceful on the hike, too.
>
> **Manuel:** I'd rather explore the campground tomorrow. We can go hiking the next day.
>
> **Father:** We can pack a lunch and have a picnic up there on top of the mountain. OK, it's decided. I think we ought to have

more of these family meetings; it's nice when we all decide things together. (Everyone gets very quiet. The enthusiasm shown by the group until then is all gone.)

Manuel: I'm going to bed.

Theresa: Me, too.

Father: Aren't we going to have a campfire? I'll play my harmonica.

Mother: No, not tonight. We're all too tired. I think I'll turn in too.

Unfortunately, the father's excitement and plans were just that—*his* excitement and plans. He didn't even hear what the others were saying. He didn't even realize that they were not having a democratic meeting. And he made his children feel that they are incapable of making their own plans—they must depend on an adult. It would have been much more meaningful if the family meeting had been conducted in a truly democratic fashion. It might have gone something like this:

Father: Now that we've got everything all set up, let's sit down and talk about some of our plans. What is it you want to do most, Theresa?

Theresa: I want to go fishing. Remember that big fish I got last year? I'm going to do it again—you'll see.

Manuel: I want to find some neat rocks for my collection. I saw a place over that way (pointing) where there are lots of rocks. I'm going to have the best collection there is.

Father: Well, I thought everyone would go for a hike with me, but I see you all have plans. What about you, Mother?

Mother: Oh, I just want to relax tomorrow. I'm so tired. I think I'll just sleep late and take care of the camp.

Theresa: Could we go on a hike later—maybe after lunch?

Manuel: Yeah, after I explore this place, I'd like to go for a hike.

Mother: Maybe I'll feel like it, too, after I get a chance to just lie around and do nothing for a while. What a change that will be!

Father: OK. Sounds good to me. I'll wait for my hike until the afternoon. It will be fun to go together.

Manuel: Hey, Dad. How about a campfire? Are you going to tell us a ghost story?

Mother: I love you all. Come on, sit here by me.
(And so they're well on their way to a happy vacation, each being considerate of one another, with respect shown for individual choices.)

By listening to your children and giving them honest choices, you can help them grow in their understanding of the democratic process. Giving many small choices will add to their feelings of self-worth and satisfy much of their innate desire for control. Once you have helped your children appreciate their ability to make choices, it will be easier for you to give choices as a means of intervention—that is, as a technique for Nondiscipline Discipline.

If your children are given opportunities to make choices in their early childhood years, they will learn to be more tolerant of others because they will recognize there are alternative ways of doing things. As they grow older, they won't find it necessary to listen to everyone who seems to be a leader. Rather, because of their home experience, they will be able to discriminate better between good and bad leadership; they will know when to follow, when to choose another option, and when to take the lead.

When there is no choice

Just as important as helping children make choices is helping them recognize that there are times when you can't give them a choice. You need to be clear and explicit in saying, "This is what has to be done." For example, explain, "Because of the weather, there is no choice today," or "Some other time you can have a choice. But because it's raining out, you have to wear these shoes today." Your children will be understanding if they learn why there is no choice: "I'm sorry, I didn't go to the store today as I had planned. This is the only kind we have. There just is no choice tonight." When there is no choice, be sure to tell your children the reason why.

CHAPTER SEVEN

Alternatives: Communication with Children

What we say and how we say it are critical in dealing with our children. The ways we communicate with them, both verbally and nonverbally, are, generally speaking, under our control and thus can be used as tools for guidance. The three alternatives described in this chapter concern what we say to children, how we say it, and how they are likely to respond.

Give Praise or Compliments

Every human being responds to genuine praise and compliments, which connote respect, admiration, caring, and appreciation. When others reassure us that we are appreciated, worthwhile, liked, capable, and accomplished, our self-esteem increases. When we make mistakes, however, we may feel guilty about not having lived up to our own or others' expectations. Dwelling on our mistakes can make us feel like failures; the resulting lowered self-image can foster tension and confusion and such behaviors as clumsiness, aggression, and withdrawal. Dwelling on children's accomplishments, no matter how small, and giving them recognition and approval affirms their worthiness and potential. It helps them develop serenity in their attitude toward living up to parents' expectations for them. Children who are constantly criticized begin feeling that they may as well give up trying, that they have no hope of achieving success and praise. Such children may test—that is, try to prove—their unworthiness by behaving even more badly than they had in the first place; they try to live up to what they feel are parents' expectations of them. Misbehavior often increases when such children receive empty praise—praise that tells them how wonderful they are when they know they have disobeyed or failed to meet an expectation.

The following considerations will help you develop the habit of using praise and giving compliments as an alternative to dictatorial and critical attitudes:

- Praise must be sincere, not condescending. Don't say "That's a beautiful design" if you think it's ugly. You could say, "I see you used some interesting shapes," or "That yellow looks bright next to the black," which are positive, honest comments that do not evaluate the picture.

- Praise should be given in as few words as possible. If you say, "Oh, how wonderful! Isn't that great? You really did that very nicely. That really was well done," the gushiness overwhelms the praise. A simple statement about feelings is easier for your child to accept: "I'm happy about how well you did. You should feel very proud."

- To be meaningful, praise should not be overused. Praise too often repeated loses its value. Concentrate on behavior that shows new steps in growth, development, or learning. Once you've complimented your child for a particular achievement, you don't have to repeat the compliment every time the act is repeated. For example, if you tell your child every day, "You made your bed nicely. I'm so proud of you. You're my best bed maker," the child may eventually reply, "You already told me." Tired of being told how proud you are of him, he will be just about ready to stop making his bed in the morning. A more effective statement might be "I see that you've finished making your bed. You may watch TV for a little while until breakfast is ready." The made-up bed is duly noted but not praised. The child has already learned that he can please you by making the bed, and it makes him feel proud to be able to do it without reminders.

There is one exception to this consideration. If your child has an especially poor self-image, you need to repeat a compliment many times to be convincing. Of course, if this is the case, your child undoubtedly has other special needs that require your special attention.

- Praise should not be confused with flattery. Praise should be something you give to someone; flattery is something you use to trick or coax something out of someone.

- Praise should be given for the efforts that your children make, not for innate intelligence. If you say, "How did you do that so quickly? You're pretty smart. I don't know how you do it," you don't give your child an impetus for future action. But if you say, "I like the way you figured out what you wanted to do and then went right ahead and finished it. That was hard," you give encouragement to try other difficult tasks.

- Praise should be given for what your children *do*. "It was very helpful to me that you behaved so nicely in the market" is preferable to "You've been my best boy today."

- Praise should be given for what your children may accomplish rather than for what they acquire. To say "Oh, what a beautiful doll Aunt Martha sent you. You certainly are lucky" emphasizes the doll. Compare it with this statement, which focuses on your child's conduct: "I can see by the gentle way you're holding that doll that you're going to be a good parent."

- Although many tasks require comformity, your children should be praised when they display originality and creative thinking. If you say, "That's not the way I showed you to make a tree," your children will sense your disappointment. But if you say, "It's exciting to see how you can make your own kinds of trees," the children will grow with their creativity.

- Praise should always be given directly to your children rather than to others within hearing. Announcing to your spouse "Aren't they doing nicely?" puts your children in the position of eavesdropping and withholds from them the pleasure of being honestly complimented. If you say to your children, "I'm pleased by the way you are doing your homework so carefully," or "I'm happy to see the way you cleaned your rooms," their self-esteem gets a boost, and they double their efforts.

- Praise should be given discreetly. Praise should not be an embarrassment to your children, and it should not imply the inadequacy of others. If you have guests in the home and you say to your child, "Show our guests that beautiful picture you just made," and then say to your guest, "He's such a good artist," your child will feel embarrassed. Instead, if you compliment your child privately, you may be able to give critical insight as well as praise without embarrassing your child.

Touching children when you give praise

When you praise your children, especially if they suffer low self-esteem, touch them gently. A gentle pat on the arm while you give a compliment will invoke the feeling of being complimented and will convey your approval. In the future, the touch alone will remind them of forgotten capabilities.

Praise for the hard-to-praise child

Some children are so negative in their behavior, and so much time is spent in conflict, that you may feel there is nothing to praise them for. These children may be so accustomed to being criticized for their antisocial and antagonistic behavior that they feel it is the way you expect them to act. They may try hard to live up to those expectations by continuing such behavior. You may eventually reduce the child's negative behavior if you do your best not to reinforce it. Don't give it any attention; instead, give attention to positive bits of behavior, no matter how small. It's important that you determine what your children do best and create many opportunities for them to do those things. Be sure you give praise when they do even the slightest things in a positive manner so that you can accustom them to the idea that your expectations are positive and within their reach.

Brian, age six, is a good example of a hard-to-praise child. He was a morose, troubled child who frequently misbehaved. He was very antagonistic toward his four-year-old brother, refused to respond when his parents made simple requests, and was having a great deal of difficulty with his behavior at school. Having been told that clay modeling provides a good emotional release for children, his mother bought several kinds of plasticine and moist modeling clay for him. She didn't say anything about it, knowing that he would then possibly react negatively and refuse to use it, or perhaps even discard it. She simply placed it on a couple of plastic trays and put it in his room. It turned out that Brian became interested in the clay, although he had always refused to touch it at both nursery school and kindergarten. At home, he began exploring what he could do with the clay. He began to make small, appealing animal shapes that delighted everyone who saw them. The compliments he received were sincere, and they led him to spend more and more time using the clay. He began to show a change in his own self-esteem, walking straighter and cooperating with his parents, and he even showed an improvement in his school behavior. He brought some of his figures to school, and the teacher arranged to have them on display. The attitude of the other children became more positive toward Brian, so that mutual feelings of awareness began to develop. As the other children became more friendly toward him, Brian's behavior continued to improve.

His parents wisely followed up the ego-boosting experience of the clay modeling by pointing out to Brian that he was really good at doing things with his hands. They gave him tasks to do around the house that required small-muscle coordination, and were always sure to let Brian know how much they appreciated his skills. They were able to help Brian develop from a brooding, antisocial youngster into a creative, cooperative family member.

When you're not used to giving praise

As difficult as it is for some children to accept praise, it is also difficult for some parents to give praise, even when it is deserved. Parents are sometimes so overwhelmed by the negative actions of their children that they find it difficult to acknowledge the positive actions. In such cases, it's a good idea to start out making some very simple requests, for which you can thank your children when they comply. For example:

- Say, "If you're finished with dinner, please take your plate to the sink for me." Be sure then, when the task is done, to say, "Thank you. That saves me some work."

- Say, "I'm going to my room to rest for a little while before I start fixing dinner. I'd appreciate it if you'd play quietly for a little while." Make the resting time very short so that you're sure your children can comply. In a few minutes, say to them, "I really liked the way you were quiet."

- Say, "Please turn the sound down on the television just a little." Then say, "Thank you for doing as I asked."

- Say, "Please wipe your shoes on the mat before coming in." Again, say, "Thank you for doing as I asked," or you could say, "Thank you for being such a good listener."

I've praised hard-to-praise children for walking straight, for turning book pages carefully, or for walking quietly. These may seem to be too minute to justify praise, but sometimes you have to strive to find a child's positive behavior! The principle is to accustom both you and your children to higher expectations; then show appreciation when attempts are made to live up to those expectations.

Acknowledging feelings of approval

Another way to expand your use of praise is to think in terms of feelings. Acknowledging feelings, both yours and your children's, is a type of praise that helps children become aware of a kind of acceptance and approval that bears no recriminations or reflection on past actions. Instead, it gives them positive feedback on the directions in which they are making positive growth. Using feelings as a basis for giving praise helps children recognize their power to develop positive patterns of action. Establishing a climate in which such praise is given sincerely can help minimize the frequency of antisocial behavior.

The following examples show how children can be complimented through the acknowledgment of feelings:

Child's Action	Your Feelings	Praise You Can Give
Suzy gives you a big smile.	Suzy always makes you feel good when she smiles.	Suzy, your smile always makes me feel good.
Tommy walks into the kitchen with a confident, erect posture instead of his usual slouch.	You imagine that he's having a good day. He feels good about himself today.	Tommy, you have very nice posture. You look like you're feeling good today.
Five-year-old Amy brings her younger brother to you for removing a splinter.	You're proud of Amy's concern for her brother's comfort.	Amy, thank you for helping your brother. I'm very proud of you.
Six-year-old Elliott pours his own glass of milk from a one-gallon container for the first time.	You feel happy that Elliott is capable of helping himself.	I'm glad that you've learned to pour your own milk.
Louise gives Sharon one of her paper dolls when Sharon's gets torn.	You are touched to see that Louise is so generous.	I like the way you share with your sister.
You go into your children's room to tell them to put away their toys and find they've already done it.	It pleases you to see how dependable your children are becoming.	I'm happy that you've put away your toys without being asked. You really are learning to be responsible.

Praising effort and accomplishment

When you and your children are comfortable with giving and getting praise through acknowledgment of feelings, you can begin to supplement that type of praise with simple statements of fact about particular accomplishments or efforts. The following are examples of statements that convey praise and emphasize feelings of approval:

To the child helping to pick up the pinto beans his brother accidentally spilled all over the kitchen floor:

Typical Response	Giving Praise and Compliments
Aaron spilled those. You don't have to help him pick them up, Joe. It's about time he learns that we're not his slaves. Besides, he should be more careful. He's always spilling things.	Joe, it's very considerate of you to help Aaron pick up all of those beans.

To the four-year-old who asks her mother to button her sweater:

Typical Response	Giving Praise and Compliments
When are you ever going to learn to button your own sweater?	Thank you for putting on your sweater. I'll button it for you, but I'll leave the bottom one unbuttoned. I think you might be able to button it. Here, just push it through this hole. That's right. You did it. That was hard.

To a child who started to use some unacceptable language but stopped himself after one syllable:

Typical Response	Giving Praise and Compliments
You had better watch your language around here. I won't stand for street talk in this house. A person would think you were raised in the gutter.	I noticed how you stopped yourself when you started to say the wrong kind of word. Thank you.

To an eight-year-old who is not a very good student and who usually forgets the homework assignments:

Typical Response	Giving Praise and Compliments
Well, it's about time you remembered to bring your spelling words home. You're the most irresponsible person I know.	I'm glad you remembered to bring home your spelling words. If you'd like, I can help you study them after dinner tonight.

The typical responses in these examples serve to punish the children and make them feel guilty. The responses that give praise and compliments encourage children to learn and develop positive behavior. They also show parents' understanding of their children; some children need more time than others do to develop motor-coordination skills, self-discipline, and responsibility, for example.

Nonverbal and indirect praise

Verbal compliments are not the only way of giving praise. There are many nonverbal and indirect methods that you can use to build and reinforce your children's good feelings about themselves. It is essential when you give praise or compliments—whether verbal or nonverbal—that you communicate your high estimation of your children's actions or potential. To express nonverbal compliments:

- Smile approval at your child.

- Nod approval at your child.

- Physically demonstrate your approval of what your child is doing by a squeeze, a hug, a gentle pat on the shoulder, or a soft stroking on the arm.

To express praise indirectly:

- Give your child a leadership task.

- Give your child a very difficult task, knowing that he or she will be able to accomplish it.

Offer Encouragement

Encouragement is closely related to praise and compliments. It provides another way for you to convey respect to your children; it is a way of saying that you appreciate their efforts and that you value them for what they can accomplish at their own levels, not in comparison to others. Encouragement bestows motivation. It renews energy, self-esteem, courage to attempt or continue difficult tasks, and independence to reach out for new levels of achievements.

Because our world is filled with uncertainty, even under the most ideal circumstances, our children are prone to self-doubt. Our goal should be to promote our children's independence of action, self-confidence, and awareness of their own capabilities. We need to think of child-rearing in terms of producing courageous persons who can face the vigorous challenges of a rapidly changing society over which hangs the threat of a nuclear holocaust. Through encouragement, we can help our children learn to surmount their problems. We can acknowledge the difficulty of a situation and help them learn that, through perseverance, industry, and practice, they can overcome obstacles.

In giving encouragement, you can help your children set realistic goals for themselves based on their individual capacities and personalities. You can help them learn that sincerely to do their best is a valid goal. Such learning will keep them from giving up when things seem to be getting more difficult. They will gradually build their skills in accordance with their growing capabilities, acquiring self-respect and strength of character at the same time.

Encouragement should be based on what you observe to be children's efforts or struggles. It should be based on what is happening at the time; it should not be judgmental or tied in to past failures. Look at what is going on at the moment and address your comments to that.

Disparaging remarks, sarcasm, and denial will make your children feel worthless. They may develop hostile and belligerent attitudes and feel so discouraged that they'll give up trying to achieve goals. The following examples show how encouragement can be used as a method of discipline and guidance:

	Typical Response	Offering Encouragement
To a child trying to tie his shoes:	Hurry up. Finish that. Use both hands. It's so easy. (This is not an appraisal of the child's efforts.)	That's very hard. Take your time. Let me know if you need help. (This acknowledges the difficulty of the task as well as the belief that the child can succeed.)
To a child trying to smooth the bedspread while making the bed:	Come on. You can do it. I don't understand why it's so difficult for you. Adrienne was able to do it when she was your age. (This comment implies that Adrienne is "better.")	That takes a lot of practice. Adrienne had to try many times before she finally learned to do it. (This gives the child hope that, through practice, she can learn and succeed.)
To a child doing homework:	Everyone can do that. I don't understand why it's so difficult for you. Those are the easiest kinds of problems. (This belittling remark implies there is something wrong with the child.)	I used to have trouble with those kinds of problems, too. Just do as many as you can, and then I'll help you with the ones you weren't able to do. I appreciate how hard you're trying. (This encourages the child to do difficult things.)
To a child practicing throwing a softball to a friend:	Why don't you watch what you're doing? Can't you see you're throwing the ball right over the flower bed? If you can't do it right, you should play something	Learning to throw balls where you want them to go takes lots of practice. Maybe you could stand just a little bit closer together, and then move back gradually. (This

Typical Response	Offering Encouragement
else. (This implies that the child is stupid and incapable.)	encourages the child to practice as well as giving a helpful suggestion for success.)

	Typical Response	Offering Encouragement
To a child screaming because she saw a spider:	That's silly. You don't have to be afraid of a little thing like that. Come here now. Look at it. I'm going to put it in this jar so you can learn not to be so afraid. (This denies the child's fear and does not help her overcome it.)	It's all right to be afraid. Some spiders are poisonous, and it's important to be careful. I'll put the spider in this jar and we can study it to learn if it is poisonous. We need to handle the jar very, very carefully. (This puts the most positive light on the child's fear.)
To a child being introduced to some visiting relatives she has never met:	Come on now. Speak up. You just get right out here and talk to these people. They've come a long way. I'm ashamed of you. Stop acting like that. Get out here, I say, or you'll be sorry. (The child cowers in a corner; the parent denies the shyness and makes a threat. It does not help overcome a legitimate problem.)	Sometimes people are shy when meeting people they've never seen before. You can talk to them later after you get used to seeing them here. (This relaxes a shy child's anxieties. It is more apt to help the child approach the guests after a little while.)
To the child who had been asked to pull some weeds in the garden:	Well, you got that far; you'd be able to finish if you weren't so lazy. I don't know how you expect to get anywhere in this life! (This belittles the child's efforts and character.)	It was hard to get as far as you did, wasn't it? But it sure looks nice. Why don't you take a little break and then start plugging away again? You have done a lot already. (This acknowl-

	Typical Response	Offering Encouragement
		edges what has already been done and encourages perseverance.)
To the child who drops and breaks a stack of dishes while helping to clear the dinner table:	I told you that you wouldn't be able to do it. Now, see the mess you've made? (This dwells on the child's error and causes humiliation, compounding the problem.)	That really was too many to carry, but I know you were trying to be helpful. Next time, make two or three trips instead of carrying them all at once. There's plenty of time. (This acknowledges the child's error but also good intentions; it offers a solution to the problem, too.)
To the child having difficulty putting on a sweater over a long-sleeved shirt:	Here, give me that. I'll put it on you. I don't think you'll ever learn to do things properly. (This denies the child's independence while belittling him at the same time.)	That's hard to put on over your long sleeves, isn't it? Here, I'll show you how to hold the sleeve so you can slip the sweater over yourself. (The parent's willingness to help prevents the child's frustration and encourages independence.)
To a child who has lied about taking her brother's pen:	If you don't tell the truth right now, in front of the family, you'll just sit here in this chair until you do. I don't care if you sit here all night. (Threats and punishment overwhelm the child and cloud the original problem.)	When we make mistakes, it's embarrassing to tell others about it. If I hold your hands and tell you I really am glad you're my little girl, will that make it easier for you to tell me why you took Derek's pen? The door is closed and no one else can hear us. (Reassurances

	Typical Response	Offering Encouragement
		and privacy encourage this child to talk about a problem.)
To a child mourning a dead pet:	Now it's been two weeks since Blackie died. Enough of this nonsense. I don't want to hear another word about it. What's gone is gone! (Lack of sympathy shames the child.)	I know you're still sad about your dog, and you will be for a long time. You loved him very much. But right now you need to do your homework. When you're finished, we can talk about Blackie again; we can talk about how much we both miss him. (Your empathy consoles the child, at least long enough for him to do his assignments.)
To a child who is fearful of riding on a bus, but must take a bus trip with the class:	I don't care how you feel. You're going on that trip with your class, and I don't want to hear anything more about it. (This denies the importance of the child's own feelings.)	I know you don't like to go on the bus. Sometimes it can be scary. It's all right to be upset. But I talked to your teacher about it, and she's going to let you sit in the front seat, right next to her. (This acknowledges the child's feelings and encourages cooperation.)

Encouragement, like praise, must be sincere. Don't pretend something is difficult when it's not: that says to your children that you don't think highly enough of them to be honest, that you think they are incapable and unworthy. Use encouragement to allow your children the pleasure of knowing that some things are indeed easy for them to do.

Also, let them feel the security of knowing that when something is difficult, you will acknowledge the difficulty and provide support or assistance.

As with praise, encouragement need not always be verbalized. A nod, a smile, a touch of the hand, standing nearby with an encouraging look on your face—all of these signals can give your children the courage to continue a difficult task. Your tone of voice, too, can convey your true feelings; so when giving encouragement, be sure that your voice carries the meaning you are trying to convey.

Clarify Messages

Clarifying messages is an important alternative method of discipline. Not only does it mean good communication, but it can prevent misunderstandings. Clarification means that when you request things of your children, you do so in clear, precise terms that leave no room for misunderstanding. Compare the following examples:

Unclear Message

This room is a big mess. (Five minutes pass.) I said, this room is a big mess. Didn't you hear me? I hope you know what that means. (The child is supposed to infer that the parent expects the child to clean up the room. Small children's minds don't work that way, so another five minutes later we hear the following.) I told you this room is a big, stupid mess. I want you to pick up all of your toys and put them where they belong right this minute. And don't expect any dessert tonight, because you certainly aren't going to get any. I sure am disgusted with you. (The parent finally gives a complete message but, by now, is so angry that punishment is inflicted. As usual, the punishment bears no relationship to the request.)

Clear Message

I expect you to pick up all of those toys and put them where they belong right now, because it's just about dinnertime. (Five minutes pass.) You've done a good job of cleaning the room. I appreciate that. Thank you. (Positive feedback is given for a job well done.)

Unclear Message

How many times do I have to tell you kids not to jump on your beds? You know that it's dangerous. Besides, you're going to ruin those mattresses. You must think money grows on trees. Now look, I told you it was dangerous: I don't care if your chin is bleeding. Go in the bathroom and wash it off. Don't come to me for help. (This parent is confusing a dangerous activity with how much things cost, thus losing both lessons on the children. They will, no doubt, jump on the mattresses again in the near future.)

Clear Message

Stop jumping and get off of those beds right now. Let's have a clear rule in this house: you may not jump on the mattresses. I worry that someone will fall and get hurt. (The message and the reasons are clear and precise.)

Get your children's attention

Before you make any requests, be sure you have your children's attention. You can do this by saying directly to them, "Look at me right now. I want to tell you something." Or you can develop various signals such as clapping your hands, turning lights off and on, using a metal whistle, or counting to three (or five). If you fail to get their attention, you'll find yourself repeating requests over and over again. When you become angry enough, your voice will rise to a pitch that your children will recognize as your own particular breaking point, and you will finally get their attention. They will listen to you, but you may be so emotional by then that your effectiveness will be lessened.

Use language your children can understand

In making requests, be sure that your children can understand what you are asking. Consider their individual abilities and development. Don't expect your three-year-old to respond with the understanding of your five-year-old. And don't expect your four-year-old to respond with the logic of a seven-year-old. Keep your words as simple as possible. State exactly what you want your children to do. Be explicit. If you want them to move their toys out of the living room, say so. If you want them to comb their hair and wash their faces, say so. If you want them to listen carefully to what you are saying, tell them so.

Give a time element

Children must also understand exactly when you expect your request to be acted on. Be specific. Use phrases like "Right now," "In five minutes" (provided they know how long five minutes is), "After lunch," "Before you go outdoors," "Before you watch TV," "Before the cartoon show," "When our company arrives," and similar explicit statements.

Consider developmental capability

Children are often asked to do things that they have not yet learned, or that they are not yet developmentally capable of doing. For example, although many children can learn to tie their shoes before five years of age, it is generally a five-and-a-half-year-old's accomplishment. It takes until approximately three years of age for children to develop good control of their shoulder muscles and the muscles leading from the shoulder to the wrist; it takes another two to two and a half years (or to about age five and a half) for them to develop fingertip control.

Frequently asking your children to do things that they are not physically capable of does not give them appropriate challenges. Instead, it can be discouraging, create poor self-images, and lead to patterns of poor response even when the tasks become easier to accomplish. You need to find a balance between what your children are already able to accomplish and the next challenging—but attainable—step in growth.

Consider intellectual capacity

Some children may indeed be physically ready for certain tasks, but they may not be ready intellectually. Some children are slower than others in processing information. A child may have a mild learning disability bordering on autism (the inability to process language), or even some strong emotional problem that interferes with the ability to concentrate on what is being said. Parents who know and understand their children will take these kinds of factors into consideration when they make requests and will gear such requests to levels their children can understand.

Use consistent wording

Be consistent in the type of wording you use for certain routine or everyday requests. Consistent wording can save a lot of misunderstanding between you and your children. If you develop certain stock phrases, your children will be able to respond to them with relative ease because they will have heard those particular requests over and over again. Some stock phrases a parent might use are: "It's beddy-bye time," "Hit the sack," "Chow time," "Up and away," "House-beautiful time" (for "Let's clean up"), "Old rags for sale" (meaning "Pick up your clothes and hang them up right now"), and similar phrases. Using stock phrases for routine tasks can free you to consider exactly how meaningfully you can word requests for nonroutine tasks. Also, consistency gives security to children who live in a world of rapid changes.

Give nonverbal reinforcement

Use body language to reinforce your verbal messages. For example, lean forward slightly to show your interest. This is especially important if you are now trying to establish appropriate response habits in your children, but they have not been accustomed to responding to your requests. To avoid being defied or ignored by your children, it is important that you look directly in their faces. If you are speaking to your children and one of them is not listening, you might say, "I'm talking to you, too."

If your children have difficulty responding to your requests, try touching them gently on the shoulder or arm when talking to them. This increases their sensory awareness. As the brain receives the touching message, other areas of the brain become more alert, and you are more apt to get an immediate response.

Be patient and understanding

Your patience will help your children learn to respond to your requests without balking or arguing. Show them that you understand it takes a long time to grow and that they are not always capable of giving an immediate response.

Sometimes it may be important to acknowledge your children's feelings verbally at the same time you let them know your expectations. You might find it helpful in some situations to express your own feelings about a particular request you are making.

Help children learn the art of clarification

Communication and human interaction are two-way streets. While you are improving your own skills in telling your children exactly what you want and when, you can help improve their clarification skills, too. Some of their skills will develop as they imitate your modeling, but you can help them further by having them practice giving you messages that state exactly what they want to tell you. Have them practice getting your attention, giving time elements, and using consistent wording in their requests. These are all important aspects of a clear message.

You can make up clarification games to play with children; for example, give a garbled message and have them try to clarify it. Older children can play the same kind of game, with the children themselves making up the garbled messages. For example, "Eggs today bought store at I the" means "I bought eggs at the store today," and "Ready o'clock at dinner six be will" means "Dinner will be ready at six o'clock."

The following are examples of messages that can easily be misunderstood. Read the first three examples. Then practice making up clear, precise messages to complete the remaining examples.

Unclear Message	What You Want	Clear Message
Get ready so we can go to the store. ("Get ready" is not a specific request.)	You want her to put on her coat.	Put on your coat so we can go to the store.
Those books don't belong on the floor. (This is a statement, not a request.)	You want him to pick up the books and put them on the shelf immediately.	Please put those books back on the shelf right now.
How dare you. That's not very nice. (The child may wonder what is not very nice.)	You want her to stop spitting at Tommy right now.	Stop spitting at Tommy right now.
I'll just wait until you're both quiet. (No time limit is given.)	You want him to be quiet right now.	_____ _____ _____

Unclear Message	What You Want	Clear Message
People aren't going to like you if you keep acting like that.	You want her to stop bothering her sister while you're reading to them.	_____ _____ _____
You'll have to miss lunch if you can't straighten up.	You want him immediately to stop throwing the ball in the house.	_____ _____ _____
Why don't you grow up and act your age?	You want them to stop jumping on the bed this minute.	_____ _____ _____
I'm certainly ashamed of you!	You don't want your child to use vulgar language.	_____ _____ _____
Can't you see you're bothering me?	You want him to wait until you're through putting some clothes in the dryer before you look at the broken car.	_____ _____ _____
You must think this family is made of money.	You want her to take her bike into the garage instead of leaving it on the sidewalk when she's through with it.	_____ _____ _____

CHAPTER EIGHT

Alternatives: Showing Restraint

Have you ever found yourself feeling oblivious to annoying or provocative behavior that usually bothers you? We don't usually think of that kind of attitude shift as being a method of guidance—but it can be. You can exert a great deal of influence over specific behaviors exhibited by your children if you respond in a flexible manner or refuse to respond to that behavior. The three "magic list" alternatives described in this chapter concern exerting control through restraint.

Overlook Small Annoyances

The more you monitor someone's behavior, the more mistakes that person is apt to make. It's important to recognize that your children need a certain amount of freedom in which to explore their relationships with others; their reactions to different environments; and their methods of expressing nervousness, impatience, boredom, or discontent. It's important that you appreciate their struggles as your children explore the world of interpersonal relationships to find out where they feel most comfortable in that world. Also, keep reminding yourself that the behavior you model for them is the behavior they will learn.

If you analyze the kinds of problems that generally occur when young children attempt to learn about interpersonal relationships, you will find that they fall into predictable categories:

1. Your child wants what someone else has.

2. Another child wants something your child has.

3. Your child strongly wants to do something in particular.

4. Your child doesn't want to do what others are doing.

In each of these conflicts, the child's response might translate, "I want to be in control." In other words, young children have difficulty sharing, following directions, or agreeing on activities to pursue together.

Practicing social skills

Children need many opportunities to learn to work out these kinds of problems among themselves if they are to develop appropriate social skills. It's important for you to distinguish between behavior that calls for immediate intervention and behavior that is just part of normal developmental exploration of control. Making such a distinction can greatly reduce the number of times you need to assume the role of police officer.

Commenting on children's behavior

When you comment on your children's behavior, it is generally your intent to change the behavior. But undue attention to a behavior often reinforces it. It is better to overlook small issues than to blow them up into big ones.

Overlooking minor incidents

Learn to overlook minor incidents, many of which your children can solve themselves; in other words, don't pick on every little action your children take. Instead, help them to work gradually to achieve healthy self-control, social skills, and self-esteem. Allow them the privilege of exercising their ideas without constant interference. Ideas and the flow of imagination work hand in hand; they need to be cultivated, not squelched. Monitoring every little thought expressed will squelch future thoughts. Learn to respect the individuality of your children and appreciate their uniqueness—just as you would want others to appreciate yours.

If you get annoyed frequently

If you find yourself getting annoyed frequently over minor incidents, you may need to examine some issues at home. Is your schedule appropriate to the ages of your children? Are you taking their needs and personalities into consideration in planning family activities? Are you considering their needs for consistency, routine, and a feeling of security? Are you using enough flexibility to accommodate unique situations?

You may need to examine your parenting role. Are you in conflict with your spouse or other adults in the household? Do your conflicts revolve around the basic philosophy of child-rearing? Are you making too many comparisons with the children of relatives and neighbors? Do you have too many people telling you what you should be doing? As a result, do you find yourself nit-picking and finding fault with your children all day long? Being a parent is strenuous and demanding, but it should also be a joyous experience for you; if it isn't, it may be *your* problem, not your children's. You may need to seek professional guidance. But sometimes it can be helpful if you just learn to overlook small annoyances and save your efforts for more important situations. The following are some examples of minor incidents that may be overlooked:

Typical Response	Overlooking Small Annoyances
Kristen, why do you have to keep wiping the bottoms of the pegs each time you pick one up? They're not dirty. (Kristen is copying some very difficult designs with the pegs. This criticism only tells her that she is inadequate.)	You're putting those pegs in exactly the right places. I think I have some harder designs you can try. (This builds self-esteem.)
Can't you stop drooling? You have spit all over your chin. You did that when you were a baby, but you're too big to do that now. I wish you'd grow up. (The drooling habit is being reinforced.)	Here's a tissue to use on your chin. (The response is being appropriately helpful. This parent makes a mental note to check with the child's dentist.)
I don't know how you can read and keep tapping your foot at the same time. You're driving me crazy. I've told you a hundred times that you	I see you're almost through with that long book. You've certainly become a good reader. (The child looks up at the parent, smiles appreciatively, gets

Typical Response	Overlooking Small Annoyances
need to break that habit. Now, you stop that right this minute and don't you ever let me catch you doing it again. (Obviously, if the parent has already told the child "a hundred times," it isn't helping to break the habit.)	in a more relaxed position, and stops the foot-tapping—temporarily. Even if it didn't stop, at least it wasn't being reinforced.)

Deliberately Ignore Provocations

Deliberately ignoring provocations is an alternative method of discipline that can be used gradually to eliminate an undesirable pattern of behavior. Children who are chronic offenders are usually already convinced that the only way they can get attention is through negative actions, aggressive behavior, or both. Unfortunately, these children are usually harangued so often that it becomes a way of life for both them and their parents. These children expect to be criticized; when they want attention, they will usually perform in a way that will evoke criticism. They have generally found that it's easier to get attention that way than to perform in a more positive, normal manner. These children are also punished frequently. Thus, the very behavior that is criticized is also reinforced, by both the attention and the punishment. Not only do these children expect to be criticized, but their parents expect to criticize them. Inadvertently, the parents spend their time looking for faults and will start haranguing their children for the most minor things.

Eliminating patterns of reinforcement

When you plan to ignore certain types of behavior, you must make certain that someone else in the family doesn't come along and give the attention that you are withholding. There should be some prearranged signal to say that a particular annoying or inappropriate behavior is going to be ignored by everyone, including other children in the family. This should not, however, seem conspiratorial.

Usually when you ignore a child's misbehavior, especially aggressive actions, the other children in the family will ignore it too. Sometimes, however, the other children will point out the misbehavior by saying something such as, "Look at Arlin. See what he's doing?" You must either ignore that comment or use some means to distract the child making the comment. Sometimes, just changing the subject will be sufficient. Sometimes, however, it may become necessary to mention ignoring the misbehavior by saying, "We're not paying attention to what Arlin is doing right now."

Deliberately ignoring provocations means that you do not give any kind of reinforcement. That means:

1. You don't say anything to the child.

2. You don't look at the child.

3. You don't display an emotional reaction to what the child is doing.

4. You don't allow your body to become tense; to do so would convey to the child that you are indeed affected by the particular behavior he or she exhibits.

5. You don't talk about it afterward. You might want to talk about feelings—but not about the behavior itself.

6. You ask all other persons present to cooperate in ignoring the behavior.

7. You are careful to give the child specific attention during periods of acceptable behavior. Give deserved praise, acknowledgment, and recognition.

Temper tantrums

Temper tantrums are commonly treated by deliberately ignoring them. Even infants and toddlers learn that throwing tantrums will get all kinds of attention for them. They gain total control over their parents, who resort to pleading, loving, hugging, yelling, shouting, shaking, threatening, begging, and even crying. When none of these methods works, parents eventually realize that the best way to stop a tantrum is to stop feeding it. That means denying it even the smallest bit of attention.

You can help your children by totally ignoring their temper tantrums and, if possible, even mild displays of temper that aren't yet tantrums. Here are a few guidelines that may help you use this alternative to help your children control their tempers:

1. Ignore the child, but make yourself available to provide reassurance when the tantrum begins to dwindle.

2. With toddlers, sit on the floor three or four feet away, not looking at the child, but being available if the child comes to you for comfort. If your toddler begins to calm down, you might move a little closer—still not looking, but beginning to establish a bond. Finally, when the tantrum stops, move to your child and give hugs and reassurance.

3. When reassuring your child after a tantrum, avoid referring to what the child did or why the tantrum occurred in the first place. Talk about how the child is feeling right at the time. Say, "You look like you are feeling better," "You look like you need another hug," or just "I love you."

4. As soon as possible after a tantrum, distract your child into a busying activity—totally unrelated to the activity that brought on the tantrum in the first place. For example, if the tantrum was over getting dressed, and you really need to get your child ready to go someplace with you, switch to getting the hair combed and the room straightened up. Then quietly go back to the dressing, reversing whatever the procedure had been when the tantrum started.

5. Try to forget about the incident yourself. It merely was your child's loss of self-control and an attempt to gain control of you as a substitute.

6. One of the problems with ignoring your child during a tantrum is that your other children, your spouse, or others in the household may be watching. Thus, the child still would be getting attention. When possible, remove the tantrum-throwing child into another part of the house where there is no audience. When you do this, be sure the area you have chosen is one in which your child will be safe and can be observed by you.

Aggressive actions toward others

When your children are acting aggressive toward one another, deliberately ignoring the behavior may change it dramatically. If you have a child who tends to become very domineering while playing with others (hitting and pushing to control them), plan ahead and try the following:

1. Alert any adults and older siblings in the household that this is the day you are going to try to deliberately ignore the child's aggressive and domineering behavior.

2. Stay close enough to where the children are playing, so you can prevent other children from getting badly hurt. If another child is hurt by the aggressive child, give very obvious attention and care to the hurt child, and totally ignore the aggressor.

3. Avoid reinforcing the aggressive child's actions by talking about them. Don't even mention them.

4. Unobtrusively encourage any other children who are present to steer clear of the bully. Most of them will do this on their own when they see you ignoring the aggressive behavior. Common sense will tell them that it's OK not to let the aggressor control—and that it's safer to stay away.

5. If the bullying child wants to talk about his or her aggressive actions, which is usually the case, refuse to do so. It is another way for the child to try to gain control. Say, "It's all right to be angry with me, but I don't want to discuss what you did."

6. Refrain from giving in to the impulse to add a snide remark such as "because your behavior is so ugly."

The following are examples of typical responses to provocative behavior and of such behavior being diminished when it is deliberately ignored:

Eighteen-month-old Nicki throws temper tantrums whenever she is left alone in her playpen, which her parents do for the sake of safety. She always becomes so violent that she vomits into the playpen.

Typical Response

Mother: Oh, look what's happened. If you hadn't cried so hard, that wouldn't have happened. Oh, you poor baby. Let me pick you up and get you all cleaned up. You mustn't cry like that when I put you in the playpen. I just do it so you won't get hurt while I'm doing my housework. You don't want me to let you get hurt, do you? There, there. You don't have to cry anymore. I'll just hold you awhile and finish my work later. You know Mommy loves you. There, there.

Deliberately Ignoring Provocations

Father: Don't go in there. Once and for all, just let her cry.
Mother: But you know her; she'll vomit all over the place and sit in a big mess.
Father: I don't see how that can hurt her. Just stay away.
Mother: There, hear her vomiting? I really need to go help her.
Father: No. Stay here. There. Hear that. She's talking to herself.
Mother (peeking): She's playing with the mess.
Father: It won't hurt her.
Mother (five minutes later): Do you suppose I can clean her up now?
Father: Yes, but remember what we discussed; don't talk or comment about what she did.
Mother (to Nicki): I'll put some clean clothes on you. (She changes her clothes and cleans her face and hands without further comment. She cleans the playpen pad and puts Nicki back in the playpen. Nicki starts to cry but sees that her mother is leaving the room without looking back. She starts playing with some blocks. Her mother finishes her housework in ten minutes and comes to take Nicki out of the playpen. They laugh.
Note: It takes only one more incident to break Nicki's habit of vomiting during a tantrum, and two more tantrums before they are eliminated totally.)

Adrienne, age three and a half, keeps throwing her silverware on the floor at mealtimes and persists in eating with her hands.

Typical Response	Deliberately Ignoring Provocations
What are you, a pig or something? How dare you throw that fork on the floor. Here, use this spoon. No! Don't throw it! I don't know what I'm going to do with you. Here, let me feed you. Stop that! OK, young lady. No dinner for you tonight.	*Mother* (picking up the silverware that Adrienne has thrown, and putting it in the sink): It's all right not to want to use a spoon or fork. I don't know why I didn't think of that sooner. (Four weeks go by. One morning, the mother serves pancakes and syrup for breakfast.) *Adrienne*: Where's my fork? *Mother* (trying not to show a reaction): Oh, here it is. I'm sorry I forgot it. (Adrienne uses silverware, appropriately, thereafter. No comment is made by either parent.) *Adrienne* (ten weeks later): Remember when I was a baby and I ate with my fingers? I was a silly, wasn't I? (Adrienne, her mother, and her father all enjoy a good laugh together.)

Sara, age two and eight months, wants a book her sister Ashley, age four, is looking at. Sara tries to grab the book. Ashley holds it close to her. Sara bites Ashley on the cheek. Ashley starts screaming, and her father comes running into the room.

Typical Response	Deliberately Ignoring Provocations
Father: How many times have I told you not to bite? Bad, bad girl. I should bite you back, that's what I should do. (He takes Sara by the shoulder and looks her in the eyes.) Why did you do it? Huh? Tell me that. Why did you do it? *Sara* (screaming): I'm sorry, I'm sorry. Won't do it no more.	*Father* (ignoring Sara completely and picking up Ashley): There, there now. That really hurts, doesn't it. (He takes her into the bathroom and washes her face. Then they go into the kitchen and make an icepack with a plastic bag and ice. He applies the cold pack to Ashley's cheek while holding her on his lap.

Typical Response

Father: That's what you said this morning. I can't have my girls biting each other. Don't you ever do that again. Here, you sit over here and be quiet and just think about what you did.
Sara (screaming): I said I'm sorry. She won't let me have the book. I hate you.
Father: Don't you talk to me like that. What kind of animal are you, anyway. Wait until your mother hears about this.

Deliberately Ignoring Provocations

Sara (entering room): But I bited. I bited hard.
Father (ignoring Sara and rocking Ashley): Remember that song I used to sing to you when you were a baby? Let's see . . . (Sara runs to her room and starts crying. She soon stops crying and comes back to where her father and sister are.)
Sara: I 'pologize. I'm too big. Won't bite no more.
Father: I would like that. Thank you. (It takes only two more similar episodes for the biting to stop completely.)

Reconsider the Situation

Reconsidering a decision in front of your child is very difficult for most parents. Somehow, we labor under the myth that, once we've set a rule or established a policy, we will lose face if we admit we were wrong and change it in front of our children. So, potentially gentle, warm, loving, intelligent parents operate from a foundation of stubbornness. They refuse to reconsider decisions after they have been announced to their children. Yet, these are the very parents who, ten years later, will proclaim to the world, "My children are the most stubborn persons ever born."

Nothing is set in concrete. Reconsideration can save the day for you many a time, as it often has for me. It might be called *flexibility*. I think I learned its value from my own two children when they were quite young. One evening, in anger, I said, "Just for that, you two can't watch television for one whole week." Three days later, I said, "Come quick and see these Scottish children dancers on TV. They're really good." My children came to me and reminded me that I had said they couldn't watch television all week. I thought for a moment and said, "I was angry and excited when I said that. I apologize. If I wanted to punish you, I should have said that you couldn't watch television for just that day. I'm not angry and excited today. Sometimes we make decisions in too big a hurry, and that's not fair to anyone. Anyway, I want you to know that it's OK for people to change their minds. I also want you to know how proud I am of you for reminding me of what I had said instead of coming to watch the program without telling me, because I had forgotten about the argument we had."

Yes, it is all right for people to change their minds. Even though one of the basic tenets of sound disciplinary practice of any kind is consistency, it should not override good sense. Being consistent does not mean being stiff-necked or walking around with blinders on. It means that you are continuously alert and aware of what everyone is doing, you apply rules and use procedures democratically and with consistency, and—because you're aware—you bend or change rules when it makes the most sense or is appropriate to do so. You use your common sense and change a plan when, after reconsideration, you see difficulties that weren't apparent at first.

It is good to remember that we live in a world of contrasts: the bad makes the good seem better; the sour makes the sweet taste sweeter. Similarly, a program of carefully planned consistency can be stronger and more meaningful if it is tempered with demonstrations of flexibility and reconsideration. It bears repeating that, in raising your children, you must always remember that you are modeling ways to act. I think it may even be important to deliberately find some rule or procedure that can be changed from time to time, temporarily, for special occasions, to demonstrate flexibility to your children.

It may help to think about these things in terms of our own jobs and supervisors. Think about what it's like working for someone who is stubborn and strong-willed and who never changes a procedure, even when it obviously has gross errors. Then imagine working for someone who listens, is willing to consider reasons for a change, and may reverse a decision if the facts warrant it. Think of the difference between these two kinds of supervisors.

Breaking rules versus being flexible

Being flexible does not mean that you don't enforce rules or procedures—it is important that you do so very consistently. Rules simply may not be ignored. Every time a particular rule is broken, the person or persons involved should be made aware that it's not all right to do so. However, breaking rules and being flexible about them are two very different things.

Being flexible means that you can say (preferably in advance), "I know that the rule is not to use the front door in the daytime except in an emergency. Today, because we are all so tired, we will lift the rule long enough for us to use that door. That will save a lot of walking. Tomorrow, the rule will again be not to use the front door during the daytime except in an emergency."

Following are examples of other ways in which reconsidering a situation can foster humane, sensible handling of potentially difficult situations and conflicts.

It is a rainy Saturday. The family is all at home. Father is changing the sink fixtures in the bathroom. Both children are in the den watching a pre-holiday parade on television. Mother has called the children to lunch. They sit down to eat, and their mother goes to help their father in the bathroom. The children put their lunches on trays and carry them to the den so they can finish watching the parade while eating.

Typical Response

Mother: Oh, there you are. How dare you bring your food in here. You know we have a strict rule about that. It's bad enough having the bathtub faucet broken, but now you expect me to clean up the den after you. Get those trays out of here, right now. And don't expect me to let you watch TV anymore today after that kind of behavior. I don't know what makes you kids so ungrateful.

Reconsidering the Situation

Mother: Oh, ho! So this is where you kids disappeared to. Well, I don't blame you for wanting to watch the parade. We don't get to see many of those. You can go ahead and finish eating in here just for today. But be sure you leave the room spotless. And don't forget—we still have the rule about not eating in the den. Next time you think we ought to bend a rule, please ask me first.

It's been raining for several days. The rain stops and the children ask if they can go play outdoors.

Typical Response

Father: I don't want you kids running around out there catching colds. Besides, we have the house all cleaned up and I don't want you tracking mud in here.
Erin: But, Daddy, we've been inside for a long time. We won't get muddy. We'll . . .

Reconsidering the Situation

Father: No, it's too cold and muddy outdoors. I think you'd better find something to do in here.
Erin: But, Daddy, we've been inside all week. And you even said we were playing so nicely, and helping you and Mommy . . .

Typical Response

Father: Don't start arguing with me. I said "no" and I mean no. And don't go trying to wheedle your mother. I'll show you who's boss around here. Go to your room. You can play in there. That's what it's for.

Reconsidering the Situation

Father: Well, you're right. You have been inside a long time. I'll tell you what: if your mother says it's OK, you put on your boots and sweaters and raincoats and go on out. But remember, if it starts clouding up again, I want you to come right back in. And stay out of the mud!

In each example, reconsidering the situation shows how a potentially tense situation has been handled with fairness and maturity, and models a good approach for the children.

CHAPTER NINE

Alternatives: Responding to Inappropriate Behavior

The three alternatives discussed in this chapter all address the question of what needs are expressed by your child's inappropriate behavior. Pointing out natural and logical consequences provides children with realistic guidelines to help them choose one behavior over another and assess the consequences of their actions. Sometimes they may need a little space and quiet time in which to breathe and recover control of their feelings; at other times they simply need some demonstrative reassurance that they are cared for and loved.

Point Out Natural, or Logical, Consequences

If you have been following the "magic list" alternatives discussed this far, you are well on your way to becoming professional in your parenting skills. When you adopt Nondiscipline Discipline, you allow your children to learn many things through the natural consequences of their own actions. When your children adhere to limits and rules and cooperate with others, they are well liked and receive positive feedback through the acceptance and cooperation of others. They develop an inner awareness that they are doing well and that they are winning your approval and that of others.

By the same token, when your children ignore or overstep limits, there are other kinds of consequences. If they are under five years of age, especially if they are only two or three, they may not connect actions to their consequences. It is important that you clarify for them

the natural consequences of their behavior. Moral judgments or punitive treatment should not accompany your pointing out consequences.

Children do not begin to think logically until they are about six and a
half or seven years old. Even then, it takes years of practice to become
skilled in the use of logic. Therefore, consequences are not always
clearly understood by preschool-age children. Kindergarten-age
children will start understanding the consequences some—but not
all—of the time. By the time they are in elementary school, most
children will respond well and even learn to determine the natural and
logical consequences of their own behavior.

Great care must be taken that this alternative not become a punishment. In the following examples, the tone of voice and demeanor
of the parent pointing out the natural or logical consequences are
critical matters. Imagine how the alternative approach to each situation
would help the children modify the way they behave:

Typical Response	Pointing Out Natural, or Logical, Consequences
Bad boy. Don't touch. See what you did now?	When you touch hot things, you get burned.
See that? People don't like to play with bad boys.	Tommy doesn't like to be hit. That makes him not want to play with you.
Don't you ever listen to anyone? Look at your new party dress. You've probably ruined it. I don't know what I'm going to do with you. I give up.	Uh-oh. You took off your apron and now you have gravy all over your dress. Maybe it will wash out.
Now, look at what you did. You spilled Danielle's cocoa, and I have no more to give her. You're such a troublemaker. I don't know what to do with you.	You can share your cocoa with Danielle, because she doesn't have any now.
You can't mail this note to your grandmother. She wouldn't be able to read these stupid chicken scratches. Can't you ever do anything right? You just sit down right now and do it over again.	I don't think your grandmother would be able to read this thank-you note. Please do it over—and take a little more time.

Typical Response	Pointing Out Natural, or Logical , Consequences
Now see what you've done? I knew you'd just keep making noise until you woke the baby up. You're never satisfied, are you? I ought to make you go right to bed.	Oh, oh. The baby woke up because you were playing too loudly. Please try to keep the noise down so I can get her back to sleep. Thank you.

Pointing out logical consequences can help your children develop the self-discipline that is the goal of the entire Nondiscipline Discipline program. However, logical consequences must be separated definitely from punishment. Your demeanor and other body language, the tone of your voice, and your words will indicate if you are employing a punitive attitude. If you are, then you are reinforcing the wrong behavior, and it will probably happen again. Repeated punishments build up defiance, and your children will repeatedly misbehave simply as an unconscious means of retaliation. It's as if your children want to say to you, "I'll show you that, no matter how much you punish me, I'll still be in control."

Provide Renewal Time

Although the term may be new to you, *renewal time* is one of the oldest and most common forms of discipline and is widely used in both homes and schools. It may be most familiar in its punitive forms: "Go to your room," or "Sit down right there and don't move," or "Now don't you dare get up from there until I tell you to." The same technique, however, can be used as a means of helping children, and it can be one of the most effective alternatives to abusive discipline.

I think it matters what you call this special kind of "alone time" that is delegated to children. "Time out" is a widely used term, and is applied to many different kinds of situations. But it often characterizes punitive isolation. The term "renewal time" is easy to say and it means what it is—a chance for the inner self to become renewed, as opposed to the whole self being "out" (isolated). Specify to your children what you really want for them during their renewal time. This will prevent you and your children from seeing renewal time as a form of punitive discipline.

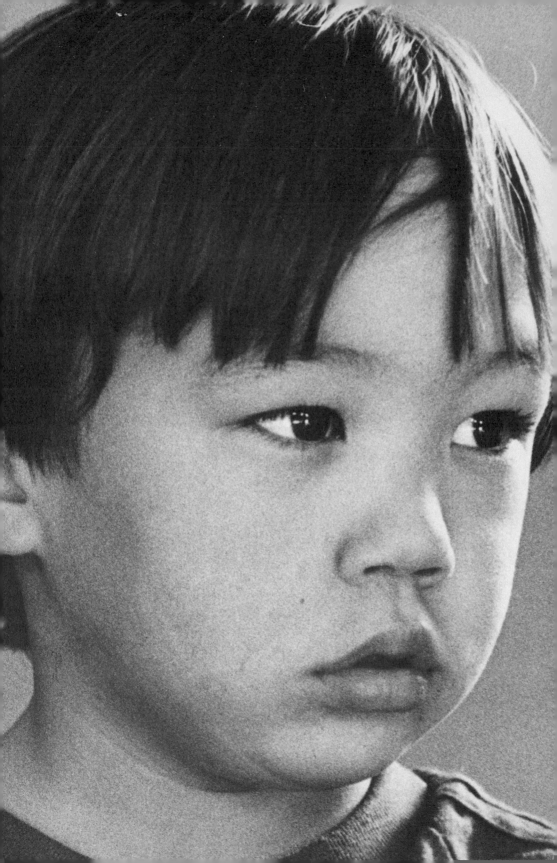

Explain renewal time to your children

It can be helpful to explain to your children exactly what renewal time is and its purpose. Tell your children that you will sometimes use renewal time when they misbehave. Tell them the truth: say that it will give them a chance to renew their feelings and will probably give you a chance to renew your feelings, too. Explain that after a renewal time, everyone just starts over.

Terminology

When misbehavior occurs and you invoke renewal time, try to gear your terminology to the time, your child, and the incident. Some phrases and directions that I have found to be useful are:

1. "Being alone for a little while."

2. "Playing quietly in your room."

3. "I want you to sit over here and have some renewal time. You may read this book. When you feel better inside yourself, you can go back to your playing."

4. "That kind of behavior simply is not allowed. I want you to go sit quietly by yourself in the den until you feel more relaxed inside yourself."

5. "I need you to go to your room for some quiet renewal time."

6. "I want you to sit right here, where no one can bother you, while you have some renewal time." (The phrase "where no one can bother you" is used to save face for a child who embarrasses easily.)

7. "You've been having trouble since you got up today. I think you need to stay in your room awhile. You can read or color in there. Come and let me know when you feel really better inside."

When you invoke renewal time, do so to give your children and yourself an opportunity to renew spirits, straighten out mixed-up feelings, regain composure, and ease inner tensions. You should learn to view renewal time as a learning experience for your children. It is a way to help your children learn to cope with the extraordinary anxieties of daily living. You don't always have to use the words *renewal time*, but you should help your children become familiar with them so that even when you use some other wording, they know what the goal is of sitting quietly alone. Your goal should be to get them into an emotional condition in which they can be cooperative rather than to punish them for already having been uncooperative.

Don't nag or recriminate

Renewal time is not a time for you to nag, shame, recriminate, give lectures, or recount other incidents of misbehavior. It's not a time for reminding children of meaningless promises, such as "I won't do it again." Talking about the behavior that caused the need for renewal time only reinforces the behavior, since it demonstrates to your child that the behavior leads to one-to-one interaction with you.

On the other hand, renewal time is not a time for saying, "You just sit there and think about what you did." When you misplace your car keys, forget to mail that important letter, or burn the toast, you certainly don't want your spouse or a child to say to you, "You just sit there and think about what you did." If you are upset about what you've done, you are already thinking about it. You certainly don't need to be told to "think about it." Sometimes, if you've made a big mistake and are embarrassed by what you did, you appreciate time to be alone for a while to recoup your feelings and your composure. Then you will be ready to take action to rectify whatever it was you did wrong. Again, it certainly won't help to be told to "think about it." Most people, when they get embarrassed or know they have done something wrong, need a cooling-off period. Children do, too.

When to give renewal time

If you want to use renewal time, it should be invoked at the time of an incident or as soon afterward as possible. If you can interrupt unacceptable behavior while it is happening (by removing the child to another area), the alone time will also serve the purpose of stopping the behavior. At this point, emotions will not yet have had a chance to build up. But if you allow a behavior to continue, by the time you've reached your level of tolerance and decided to intervene, your emotions and those of your child will have built up. In such cases, your child may even need help calming down before he or she can handle being alone. If you invoke renewal time in such instances, your child is apt to consider it a form of punishment.

How long to stay away

Children seem to sense when they have achieved the purpose of the alone time. If you are honest with your children and explain about the idea of renewing one's "inside-of-me" feelings, they will develop an understanding of how much renewal time they need. You'll find that the time needs to be adjusted for each child and also for the child's mood at the time of the incident. You may find that a renewal time of just three or four minutes is all that is necessary to give a child a chance to take an apparently much needed "inner breath." Some children may need to be by themselves for a quiet ten or fifteen minutes or even longer. A tired child will need more time alone than a rested child needs. An extremely agitated child may need more time than one who is not very emotionally excited.

Sometimes your child may not really need much (or any) time alone, but you may. Be honest. Offer some special drawing paper or a special book or other surprise that you have been saving for just such an occasion and say, "'I need some time by myself." You may even decide to go into your room for some renewal time of your own, away from the rest of the family. Ten minutes of such time, perhaps with your feet up and with total quiet, can be a great reviver.

Extinguishing a particular behavior

Renewal time is an effective method for extinguishing inappropriate behavior. For example, Rosa had developed the annoying habit of sticking out her tongue at anyone who disagreed with her or wouldn't let her have her own way. Her older brother and younger sister kept complaining about it, which probably reinforced the activity. Finally, Rosa's mother said that the new rule in the house was that people were not to stick out their tongues at one another. She told Rosa that every time she did it she would have a renewal time.

Several times during the following week, Rosa became angry and immediately stuck out her tongue at either her brother, sister, mother, or father. Each time, her mother or father said to her, "You need some renewal time. Let me know when you feel better," or "Let me know when you're not angry anymore," or "When you feel better inside yourself, you can get up from there." No comment was made about sticking out the tongue or about its not being polite. During renewal times, Rosa was allowed to read a book that her mother or father would select for her. By the fifth day, Rosa started to stick out her tongue a couple of times but caught herself and said, "I'm sorry. I didn't mean to do that." In fact, on the fifth day she was given only two renewal times. By the sixth day, she was able to stop herself every time, and the habit seemed to have been broken. Realizing the self-control she was now demonstrating, Rosa's self-esteem increased and she seemed to be a happier child. She was much more relaxed and seemed relieved to have rid herself of the habit.

Keep a nonpunitive attitude

As with the "magic list" alternative discussed earlier in this chapter (pointing out the consequences of certain behavior), renewal time also needs to be used with much care and thoughtfulness to prevent it from becoming a punishment or from reinforcing inappropriate behavior. It should be neutral. If you are really excited and angry, it is all right to say so. But once your child is in an alone place, once the renewal time is in process, there should be no overattention. By the same token, don't pretend the child isn't there. The principle is to ignore but not reject. The situation should not be unpleasant, but not so pleasant that your children will deliberately misbehave in the hopes of having a renewal time. They should be treated humanely, but not so lovingly and tenderly that renewal time becomes a treat. I once had the following experience at a nursery school:

Jim, age four, pushed Lisa, age three, off a tricycle. I immediately sent him inside and told him to sit down. I gave him a bowl of nuts and a nutcracker and said, "Please crack these for me. I need them for snack-time." I showed him how to use the nutcracker, and he went to work on the task. I stepped out into the hallway for a moment. When I came back in, I saw Lisa at the door, halfway into the room. "No," Jimmy was saying, "first you have to hit somebody. Then you can come in."

I realized I had been too welcoming in my attitude toward Jimmy. I quietly took him by the hand, guided him away from the table where he was working, and said, "I've changed my mind. I need to have you sit over here, away from the window, and just look at this book. No talking, please." But the damage had been done. In subsequent weeks I had to find ways of dealing with Jimmy other than offering him renewal time.

The following examples show how renewal time can be used as a response to misbehavior:

Lucy, age five and a half, is in her yard playing with her friend Georgia. Lucy grabs the doll buggy away from Georgia, shouting, "You can't touch that. It's mine. Go home." Her friend begins to cry.

Typical Response	Providing Renewal Time
Parent (grabbing Lucy by the arm and yanking her into the house): I'm ashamed of you. How can you be so ugly? You never see me acting like that, do you? You just sit down on this stool and think about what you did. And don't you dare move until I tell you to. I'm so ashamed of you. What will Georgia's parents think?	*Parent*: Georgia, I'm sorry that Lucy acted that way. Here, you can play with the buggy. Lucy, I think you need to sit down quietly over here on the steps until you feel better inside yourself. No one can bother you over here. (Four minutes later, her parent notices that Lucy seems more relaxed and suggests that she play with Georgia. The parent doesn't nag or remind Lucy to share. Now that Lucy is more relaxed, she presumably won't need such a reminder.)

Frank, age four, walks to a table where Lupe, age six, is playing with a new jigsaw puzzle. He stops suddenly, leans over the table, and messes up the puzzle pieces Lupe has fitted together.

Typical Response	Providing Renewal Time
Parent: I saw that. What a terrible way to act. You can't go around doing things like that to your sister. Ten minutes' time out for you. You just sit down and be quiet. One more thing like that, and you'll really be sorry. I don't know when you're going to learn to act your age.	*Parent* (in a quiet voice): You may sit quietly for a few minutes until you feel better. Here's a book to look at. (Frank is not told when to get up. He sits quietly awhile; then, feeling calmed down, he gets up and walks over to his sister.) *Frank*: I 'pologize. (The two children play happily together.)

Steven, age eight, rushes in after soccer practice and shouts, "I hate school. I hate soccer. I hate Jimmy. I hate everybody. Don't you ever make me go back to that school again!" He runs to his room and slams the door. Then he comes out again, runs over to his mother, tries to kick her, and yells, "I hate you, too."

Typical Response	Providing Renewal Time
Mother: Steven, what do you think you're doing? Just because you're excited, you don't have to come in here shouting at me like that. I'm your mother, and I'm not about to let you get away with that kind of behavior. Get back in your room and don't you dare come out until I'm good and ready to see you. And I don't want to hear any noise in there, either. (Steven runs to his room, slams the door, throws himself down on his bed, and sobs.)	*Mother*: Steven, I can't let you kick me. Now, come over here and sit down awhile and give yourself a chance to calm down. As soon as you feel better, I want to hear all about what happened. It must really have been a bad time for you. (Mother deliberately leaves the room for a few minutes. She comes back in and speaks.) Let's talk about it now. Tell me what happened. (Recognizing that Steven has had an upsetting experience, she tries to be helpful by letting him calm down a little and then tell her about it.)

Renewal time is easy to use as an alternative method of discipline, but it is also ineffective when overused. If you find that you are giving your child renewal time over and over again, it is obviously not serving its purpose. Perhaps your child has not grasped the meaning of the isolation. Perhaps some repetitive misbehavior is due to a physical condition that needs to be treated. As with all of the alternatives in this book, renewal time can be very effective but is not a panacea.

Give Hugs and Caring

Some children become convinced that the only way they can get attention (especially from their parents) is to annoy others. You can give praise and encouragement and even try to ignore the problem behavior totally, but it continues. These children may each have had some traumatic experience—such as the death of a close family member—in their earliest years. Or perhaps there is an older child in the family who gets much attention because of a chronic illness or physical disability. Often, the problem can be traced to an unpleasant or unsettled separation or divorce between the parents.

Such children need to be evaluated very carefully. When you have tried various alternatives as presented throughout this book and the child's attention-getting misbehavior continues, try giving hugs and caring. Often, what such children need is just lots of reassurance through physical contact and the demonstration of open affection. They may not need explanations or attempts at understanding.

Even normal children who do not have special behavior problems need frequent demonstrations of affection. They will respond well to hugs and to being told how much you care for them. We parents often decide that our children are too big to sit on our laps, too old to crawl into bed on a Saturday morning, or too mature to kiss goodbye before they leave for school each day or before you leave for work. In some households today, in fact, parents have a fear of being accused, wrongfully, of sexual abuse. Many children, therefore, are not getting the physical affection their inner selves are crying out for.

CHAPTER TEN

Alternatives: Dealing with Conflict

Once conflict erupts, children and their parents need to know how to resolve it without recourse to violence. Teaching your children (1) to describe their own emotions and motives, (2) to listen empathetically to what others have to say, and (3) to find common ground on which differences can be resolved is one of the most valuable things you can do for them. It is important that we use discussion techniques ourselves—to model such behavior—in settling differences that come up in the family.

Arrange Discussion Among the Children

Discussion is a legitimate and positive means of helping your children develop social skills. When they have been involved in conflict with you or with other children, when they have been behaving poorly and displaying negative behavior, they can be taught to discuss problems. Discussion can forestall arguments; your children will learn that disputes can be settled in a nonviolent manner and will have a vehicle for venting feelings.

To understand the value of helping your children learn the art of discussion, picture yourself when you have made a mistake. Do you want to be reminded critically of the mistake? How would you feel about being yelled at and berated in front of others? Would you want to be punished by not being allowed to eat your dinner or to continue interacting with friends and family? Or would you prefer to be given an opportunity to discuss the situation with whoever else was involved and to establish a plan for appropriate behavior or action if a similar situation should arise in the future?

So it is with children. Discussion gives them an opportunity to evaluate what took place and to plan an alternative for the next time. It also means that both sides can present their points of view, talk about their feelings, and come to some terms of understanding one another, even though they still may disagree.

What a discussion is not

1. A discussion is not an argument or dispute. In arguments and disputes, everyone talks about what happened and about how they felt or about what they feel is right, but no one listens.

2. A discussion is not a one-sided lecture. In one-sided lectures, only one person (usually the parent) gets to present a point of view; the others involved do not.

3. A discussion is not nagging and rehashing for the purpose of producing guilt, which is merely an alternative to saying, "You had better listen to me. I'm the person with the power."

What a discussion is

1. A discussion is when two or more persons present their individual or opposing points of view, along with their feelings about those points of view, while listening carefully to one another.

2. A discussion is an opportunity for the parties involved to evaluate what caused the disagreement and to figure out an alternative for the next time the same or similar situation arises.

3. A discussion is a means of helping your children learn to solve their own problems with the support of one another.

4. A discussion is a way of saying to your children, "Your perceptions and feelings are important, even though they may differ from mine."

5. A discussion is a way of saying to your children that you trust them.

Conversation

Conversation is the first step toward developing the art of discussion. In the context of this book, conversation means sharing information and ideas without focusing on conflict. Your children need to learn the art of conversation from you. Too often, our primary communication with young children revolves around giving commands and asking questions. They need practice and encouragement to learn to engage in two-way conversations. The following steps can be taken to help children learn to carry on conversations:

1. Choose subjects that you know your children are interested in. Your interest, if not in the subject, can be in the excitement of your children's growing capabilities as their skills at conversation grow. Look for areas of common interest to talk about, such as weekend or vacation activities, birthday parties, pets, relatives, the weather, the news, and other topics that touch the lives of both you and your children. Whatever the topic, don't talk down to them. You must converse as equals.

2. Maintain nonjudgmental interest. Don't ridicule their misinterpretation of such things as scientific facts and statistics. Rather, relish their willingness to impart information, and recognize that what they are saying is based on their points of view and their perceptions, not those of the adult world. At the same time, don't be condescending. If there is a blatant error, inquire about where the information originated without making fun of an immature concept. Realize that, as children develop perceptual skills, they go through various immature stages to gradually more mature levels of comprehension.

3. Avoid asking yes-and-no questions. Questions can be used to teach conversational skills if they are carefully worded to stimulate thought. Learn to pick up on your children's comments and ask thought-provoking questions to extend the conversation in the direction they have chosen. When you ask children about their preferences, inquire also into

the reasons for those preferences. Do not hesitate to ask for their opinions even when you know you will not agree with them. Disagreements can lead to even more conversation and to the first principles of discussion. Here are some examples of thought-provoking questions to help children learn the art of conversation:

I know you are hoping to get a dog for your birthday. What do you think it will look like? What will you teach it to do? Why is it good to have a pet?

Look how dark and cloudy the day is. Have you seen it looking like that before? What happened?

Initiate conversations that may stimulate thoughts and ideas rather than just yes-and-no answers. Even a three-year-old can be engaged in a conversation such as the following:

Mother: Can you remember two things we had for breakfast this morning?
Child: Mmmm. Oatmeal. (Pause.) I had toast.
Mother: You did tell me two things. I had three things. I had orange juice and an egg and coffee. I know I didn't give you coffee to drink.
Child: You gave me milk.
Mother: What about milk?
Child: I like it. Drink it.

4. Play conversation games:
   a. Listening. Whisper a sentence to a family member. That person whispers it to the next person. Keep going until it comes back to you. Tell everyone aloud what was told to you. Tell them what the original statement had been.
   b. Discussion story. Tell a story about a discussion you had, leaving blanks for your children to take turns filling in. For example, "Mrs. Jones and I were discussing things to remember when crossing the street. I said that the most important thing was _____ . She said, 'No, the most important thing is _____ .' I said, 'What makes you think that?' She said, '_____ .'" And so on, with this and other topics.

Discuss problems—don't argue

If you are going to teach your children to engage in discussions to settle differences, you have to make up your mind that you will not argue with them. It takes two to create an argument. In many homes, arguments are a way of life. If this is true in your home, your children will learn to question the validity of everything you do and challenge any control that you may try to exercise. They will argue with you at the slightest provocation. To make a change, you need to let your children know that you will no longer be trapped into arguments. You can say, "We can have a discussion about that." Arguing wastes the time and energy of everyone involved. Your children can be helped to recognize this fact. They will generally respond well to being taught how to convert an anger-filled argument into a legitimate discussion.

Talk with your children about the differences between discussions and quarrels. Help them learn the following rules for discussions:

1. Listen to each other and look directly at one another when you talk. If there are more than two people involved, everyone should look directly at the person who is speaking. If someone doesn't seem to be listening, the speaker should reach out and touch the person's hand and politely say, "I'm talking to you."

2. State what happened and how you feel. All of the people involved should state what they think happened, how they were feeling at the time, and how they feel about it now. Explaining feelings during a discussion is a more legitimate way of acknowledging emotional reactions than allowing the facts to be overwhelmed by emotions, as they often are in an argument.

3. Empathize with the other person or persons, even though you may hold out for your own point of view. You don't have to agree with the other person or persons, but you do have to grant others the right to express their own opinions, just as you have the right to express yours. You can demonstrate empathetic listening by leaning forward while listening, nodding in response to what someone is saying, and keeping attention focused on the speaker.

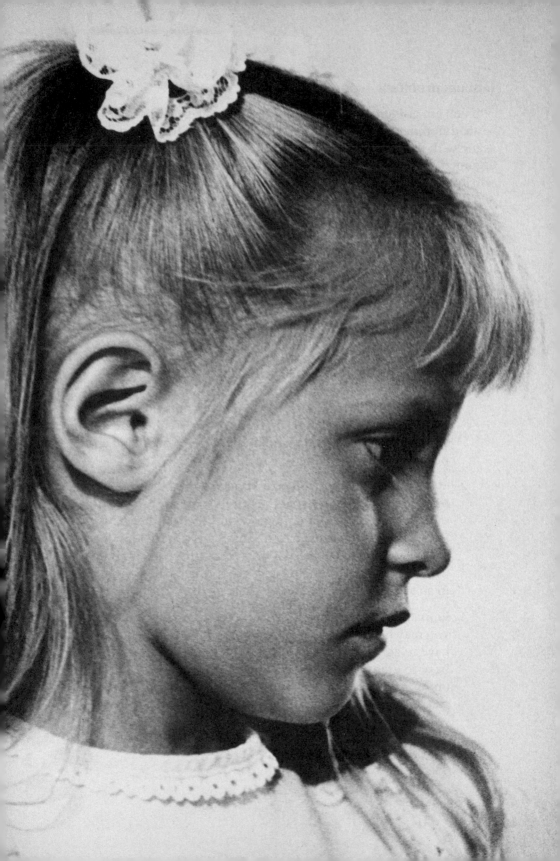

Help children to substitute discussion for conflict

If you have established an atmosphere in which your children know they are listened to, they can begin to substitute discussions for conflict. Even with children three and four years of age, take the time to get them to discuss what is happening during a confrontation. Use the technique illustrated in the following examples:

Jack, age four, is having a hard time sharing his toys with his brother Paul, age three. Jack takes his truck away from Paul, who kicks Jack in return.

> *Father* (to Jack): Tell him that hurts you.
> *Jack*: That's mine.
> *Father*: Tell Paul it hurts when he kicks you.
> *Paul*: I was playing with the truck and he took it.
> *Jack*: That's my truck.
> *Father*: You could ask Jack for it.
> *Jack*: My truck.
> *Father*: Tell Paul it hurts you when he kicks.
> *Jack*: It hurts. I don't like it.
> *Paul*: But I had it.
> *Father*: You need to ask each other for things.
> *Paul*: Can I play with it?
> *Jack*: I'll be the car man. Here, I'll give you gas.
> (And so the two start playing together.)

Amy and Susan, ages four and five, request intervention from their mother when they have a conflict.

> *Susan*: Mama, she spit at me.
> *Mother*: Go tell her you don't like that.
> *Susan* (to Amy): I don't like that.
> *Amy*: You hit me.
> *Mother*: Tell her how you feel.
> *Amy*: That hurt me.
> *Mother*: Susan, tell Amy how you feel.
> *Susan*: The spit hurt me. I don't like it.
> *Amy*: I won't do it again.
> *Susan*: Let's play we have to go to the store.
> (And they start playing happily together.)

Patience and persistence will pay off. It may take weeks of prompting and modeling, but you will finally be able to say to your children, "Just discuss it" or "You need to use your words."

As children learn to discuss problems, it is important to let them take the lead in deciding what to say and how to respond. They may still need a little prompting from you. For example, you may need to say:

- "Talk to each other. Tell what happened. Tell how you feel."

- "Listen to each other."

- "What can you do next time that happens?"

Gradually, they will carry on fruitful discussions with less and less help.

If your children are going to learn to carry on their own discussions, you must limit any prompting you give to clarifying the rules from time to time. Trust them to manage by themselves. Don't eavesdrop except to be sure the discussion is going on or to determine that help is needed. Remember that there is no one correct approach they should use to express their thoughts and feelings. The important thing is that, with your trust, they will learn to trust themselves and each other to settle differences by talking about them. As their experience grows, you can ignore their discussions more and more.

A word of caution: don't follow up a valid discussion between children with a lecture. This would convey to them that, even though they have learned to discuss their problems, they need you to sum things up. Your children will not grow to think of themselves as self-sufficient problem solvers.

The following are examples of situations in which parents foster problem-solving discussion skills among their children. Contrast this approach to the more typical responses.

Benjamin, age seven, requests intervention during a conflict with his brother Howard, age nine.
Benjamin: Mom! Mom! Howard's got my tape recorder. He won't give it to me.

Howard (simultaneously): I'm just listening to something on it. I'll be through with it in a minute.

Typical Response

Mother: Howard, you better give him his tape recorder. You don't like it when he takes your things.
Howard: But I only needed to hear this one thing. Besides, mine needs a new battery.
Benjamin: You could plug it in. You just wanna use mine. Mom, make him give it to me.
Mother: I'm sick and tired of all this bickering. I can't keep settling your arguments for you. Benjamin, stop picking on your brother.
Benjamin: But it's my tape recorder.
Howard: Yeah. He didn't even want it 'til he heard me using it.
Mother: You two boys get in your room and close the door. I'm disgusted with you. I don't want to hear any more about it.

Arranging Discussion

Mother: Don't get me involved. You boys discuss it between yourselves.
Benjamin (to Howard): Give me that tape recorder.
Howard: I know it's yours. Can I just listen to how the end of this song goes? It'll just take a minute. My recorder's broken.
Benjamin: Yeah, well, I don't like you to take my things without asking.
Howard: I didn't think you'd care. I'll be through in a minute. Can I please finish? I do lots of favors for you.
Benjamin: Well, OK. You can use it. I've got to go and see what's wrong with my bike, anyway.
Howard: I'll come and help you in a minute, as soon as I'm through.

Five-year-old Lynn hits her sister Debby, age four, during a quarrel. Debby runs to their mother for help.
Debby (crying): She hit me. Make her stop.
Lynn (simultaneously): She scribbled on my good paper. Look what she did.

Typical Response

Mother: I told you girls if you didn't behave you'd both have to take naps. Now stop that crying this minute.
Debby: But she hit me.

Arranging Discussion

Mother: Lynn, that's something you and Debby can discuss. Did you tell Debby you didn't like it when she scribbled on your paper?

Typical Response

Mother: How many times do I have to tell you not to hit each other? (She slaps Lynn.) There, how do you like that? Now, you both had better get in your room and take naps. I don't want to hear a sound out of you until I tell you.

Arranging Discussion

Lynn (to Debby): I don't want you to scribble on my stuff.
Debby: But you hit me.
Mother: Tell Lynn how that made you feel.
Debby: That hurt. I don't like that.
Lynn: But I only did it after you scribbled.
Debby: That's not fair.
Lynn: I'm sorry I hit you.
Debby: Your picture is prettier.
Lynn: But I like yours. Do you want to use my gold crayon?
Debby: Naw. I'm gonna use lots of green. I like it.
Mother: You girls finish your drawings. We're going to have dinner in about ten minutes.

Though only four and five years old, Lynn and Debby were able to tell each other how they felt. It's interesting that though only one child apologized, the mother did not interfere and make the other one do so as well. The one apology seemed to suffice for both girls. They were already liking each other better after listening to one another, and they were anxious to get back to their playing.

Even three-year-olds can be introduced to the use of discussions. In the beginning, they will communicate primarily by just looking at one another. It seems to serve the same purpose as a verbal discussion, and it sets the framework for them to grow into the ability to verbalize with one another. Here is an example:

Typical Response

Father (grabbing Donna): I see you trying to hit Bruce. That's not being a very nice girl.
Donna: He hurt me.

Arranging Discussion

Father (kneeling by Donna and putting his arms around her to hold her arms and prevent her from hitting out): I can't let you hit Bruce,

Typical Response

Father: That's no excuse for you to hit someone. Don't you dare let me see you doing that again. Now, tell him you're sorry. (Instead of helping the children learn appropriate social skills, he is demanding a one-sided apology and is not listening or teaching Donna to listen to the other side of the incident.)

Arranging Discussion

even though he hit you first.
Donna: He hit me.
Father: And that made you unhappy. But I can't let you hit someone. You and Bruce need to talk about it with each other. Just use your words.
Bruce: What?
Donna (giggling): What?
(They look at each other, giggling.)
Donna: I like you.
Bruce: Let's play.

If your children are a little older and you have never introduced them to the idea of having a discussion, a minor squabble will give you an opportunity to do so. The following example shows how:

Barbara, age six, Georgia, age nine, and Danny, age eleven, are quarreling over the ownership of some coupons for free hamburgers.

Typical Response

Mother: Danny, you're old enough to know better than that. And you two girls—I'm surprised at you. You know that if anyone gets a hamburger, you'll each get one. You'd think you kids never got anything to eat around here, or that you didn't even have an allowance. Now give those coupons to me. I don't want to know whose they are. I'll keep them. I just might decide to use them for Daddy and myself. Now, you kids get into your rooms and clean them up. And I had better not hear another word out of you. Danny, you're grounded for the rest

Arranging Discussion

Mother: Wow! You kids aren't talking very nicely to each other. I think you all need to sit down at that table over there and discuss how you can manage to share those coupons. I want you to be sure that each of you listens to what the others have to say. You can take turns telling whose coupons you think they are. I want you to tell each other how you're feeling about this quarreling, too. Remember, everyone gets a turn to talk by themselves while the others listen. (She leaves the room.)
Danny: OK, I had these in my top dresser drawer.

Typical Response

of the day. Imagine a big boy like you acting like a little kid. You're supposed to be their big brother and an example to them. I'm thoroughly disgusted with you. In fact, I'm disgusted with this whole family!

Arranging Discussion

Barbara: But Daddy gave me some. I had them.
Danny: But mine are gone.
Georgia: I didn't take your old coupons. I had my own. Barbara gave them to me.
Barbara: You're trying to get me into trouble!
Georgia: Maybe Dad will give us some more.
Danny: I've got an idea. Why don't we divide them up?
Barbara: Well, OK.
Georgia: Here, Barbara, you keep all the coupons in your box. That way we all know where they are.
Danny: We can ask Dad to drive us over to the restaurant Saturday.
Georgia: Come on, Barbara. Let's put these other things away.
Danny: I have to do my homework now.
Mother (coming back into the room): That was a good discussion you children had. I'm very proud of all of you.

Provide Discussion with an Adult

There will be many occasions when it will be more appropriate for your children to discuss a problem with you instead of with another child, especially when only one child is involved in misconduct. Your mood and demeanor in such a situation become critical factors in the success or failure of the discussion.

Take care not to allow the discussion to become a reinforcement of poor behavior. You should not drop everything you are doing to involve yourself in a three- to five-minute discussion every time you disapprove of something one of your children does. They would then learn that they need only misbehave to gain your total attention and total control over you for a period of time. Also remember that angry overreaction to inappropriate behavior also reinforces the behavior by creating, among other things, a contest of wills.

Avoid power struggles

Above all, you should avoid getting into the habit of indulging in power struggles with your children. Usually this habit gets started when children are toddlers when you're trying to help them develop habits of eating, toileting, and sleeping that will conform to your expectations. Even if you managed to avoid power struggles during those years, you need to guard against letting them develop as your children's need for independence continues to increase. By establishing good habits of family discussions, such power struggles may be avoided.

Instilling good discussion techniques

It is your responsibility to promote wholesome interpersonal relationships in your home. You will need to weigh carefully every response you make to the inappropriate actions of your children. You will need to find ways of striking a gentle balance between helping them develop independence of action and helping them develop the inner strength to monitor those actions themselves. Also remember that you are always modeling behavior they will imitate. The way you handle discussion—not only with them, but also with other adults—is the way they will learn to do so.

Not all children respond well to discussion with a parent as a method of that parent's intervention. Having direct discussions, however, can help you discover more about what your children are thinking. This, in turn, will help you figure out what other kinds of intervention each particular child might respond to best, and what kind of skill-development assistance each child might need.

Some children, on the other hand, will respond particularly well, and with great relief, to learning to discuss their feelings with you. When you discuss their behavior and feelings, make sure it isn't a lecture and that they get to do their share of the talking. Make it a true exchange of information. Criteria for a good discussion are:

1. Each person states what he or she thinks happened.

2. Each person listens to what others say.

3. Everyone states individually what they intended to accomplish by their actions.

4. Each person states how he or she felt.

5. Everyone states individually how they think others might have felt.

6. Anyone can contract for some alternative type of behavior in the future that would accomplish his or her intent by more acceptable means.

When to have the discussion

There shouldn't be any set rules about a waiting time between an incident and a discussion about it. Often, the discussion can be held immediately after an occurrence, but if either you or your child is overwrought, the discussion should wait until the emotions have quieted down. An upset child should probably have some renewal time alone to read a book, color, or do some other independent, sedentary activity. This allows the child's feelings to simmer down and permits the child to do some self-evaluation. After five, ten, or fifteen minutes, you could then approach your child, pull up a chair, and say, "Let's discuss what happened." If your child still seems to be in a heightened emotional state, your first priority should be to induce calmness. The discussion can wait until a later time. It should also be postponed if you find that you are still angry.

The following examples show ways parents can use discussion with their children to help them modify their behavior:

Rod, age six, is playing with some neighborhood friends in front of his house. His father calls him to dinner and he doesn't respond. Five minutes later, his father calls him again. He still doesn't respond. Finally, the father walks over to where Rod is playing and says, "You get into the house right this minute."

Typical Response	Arranging Discussion
Father (following Rod into the house): I'm sick and tired of our	*Father* (following Rod into the house): I want you to go in and wash

Typical Response

having to call you every time we want
you, and then you don't even answer.
I'm not going to keep making a fool
of myself in front of the whole
neighborhood and let them see that
you don't even listen to me.
Rod (simultaneously): But I was "it"
and I'd spoil the game if I didn't
finish. I said I'd come in a minute.
Father (not listening): I don't care.
From now on, when I call you, I
expect you to come the first time.
Take that, and that (as he leans over
and swats Rod on the seat a couple
times).
Rod: I hate you.
Father: Now you asked for it. You get
to your room. No dinner for you.
And don't think we'll feel sorry for
you and give you something later. It's
about time you learn some manners
around here.

Arranging Discussion

your hands for dinner. Then I want
you and me to sit down and discuss
this business of your not coming
when I call you.
Rod (after washing his hands): I
washed.
Father: I know when you're playing
you don't like to leave your friends.
But when I come home I'm really
tired. I don't like having to call you
more than once because that makes
me more tired. Then that makes me
get angry.
Rod: But I was coming. I only had to
finish being "it." I thought it would
be all right if you waited.
Father: I really need you to come the
first time I call. Your mother needs
that, too.
Rod: But what about the game?
Father: I'll tell you what. The next
time one of us calls you, if you have
to have a little time to finish a game,
why don't you just walk over to us
and tell us that? Then we'll understand, and if we can wait, we will.
Rod: That's a good idea. I'll come
when you call me.
Father: Hey, pal. Let's go eat. I smell
something good in there!

**Mother, coming home from work, walks into the living room just in
time to see Gary, age four, try to kick Anna, the babysitter.**

Typical Response

Mother: Gary, stop that. How dare
you act like that. You can't treat Anna
like that. (She slaps him in the face.)
Gary (picking up a toy truck and
flinging it across the room, just
missing the door of a glass

Discussion with an Adult

Mother (walking over to Gary,
picking him up, and setting him
down on a chair): I can't let you kick
people.
Gary: I hate you.
Mother: I can tell you aren't feeling

Typical Response

cupboard): Get away from me.
Mother: Don't you talk to me that way. (She slaps him again.)
Gary (screaming): Go away! Go away!
Mother (grabbing him by the shoulders): You look here. I'm your mother and I'm not about to let you talk to me that way. I don't know what I'm going to do with you. You get worse every day. I might decide not to come home one day. That'll teach you a lesson.

Discussion with an Adult

very happy right now. (She picks him up and takes him to his room.) I want you to stay in here and read for a little while. As soon as you feel better, and as soon as I take off my coat and relax for a few minutes, we'll talk about kicking people. (She quickly leaves the room. Three minutes pass.)
Mother: Come on, Gary, let's talk about it.
Gary: Go away.
Mother: I felt angry when I walked in the house and saw you trying to kick Anna.
Gary: I was mad.
Mother: You must have felt very mad to want to kick her. She's your friend.
Gary: She said I couldn't go play.
Mother: You wanted to go play.
Gary: Yeah. I wanted to ride my bike.
Mother: That's always fun to do. But Anna can't let you go out to ride your bike when it's dark outside. And I would be unhappy about that, too.
Gary: I don't like to ride when it's dark.
Mother: Next time, you can look out the window first and see if it's dark.
Gary: I like Anna.
Mother: And I like you.
Gary: I like you, too. I love you, Mommy.

Learning to use discussions in your household will save much time and energy and will prevent misspent emotions. Discussions can largely determine change in your children's behavior. As children begin to value discussions, their self-esteem increases, and the entire family will benefit.

CHAPTER ELEVEN

Systematic Problem Solving

The system described here is one that I have used successfully, both with teachers and with parents. The primary requirement is total honesty. Without honesty, the process will only create additional problems. Once you have determined that you can approach the system with honesty, the following steps should be taken.

1. Identify the problem. No matter what misbehaviors are evidenced, you should attempt to solve only one specific problem at a time. Often, in solving one problem, others will automatically be resolved. To begin with, pinpoint only one problem to analyze for a solution. The following steps will help you in doing so:

   a. On a sheet of paper, write out the observable facts. What have you seen or heard your child do? Are there any accompanying sensations that need to be considered? Don't surmise anything. List the date and the time that each incident occurs. List what each person involved may have said during the incident. State specific facts, such as "Tommy poked Kristy in the ribs when he was sitting next to her at the breakfast table. She cried; I shouted at Tommy; he threw his spoon on the floor and ran to his room, slamming the door after him."

   b. State the feelings you think were involved. You can only assume what others were feeling, but you can be sure of your own feelings. For example, "I was

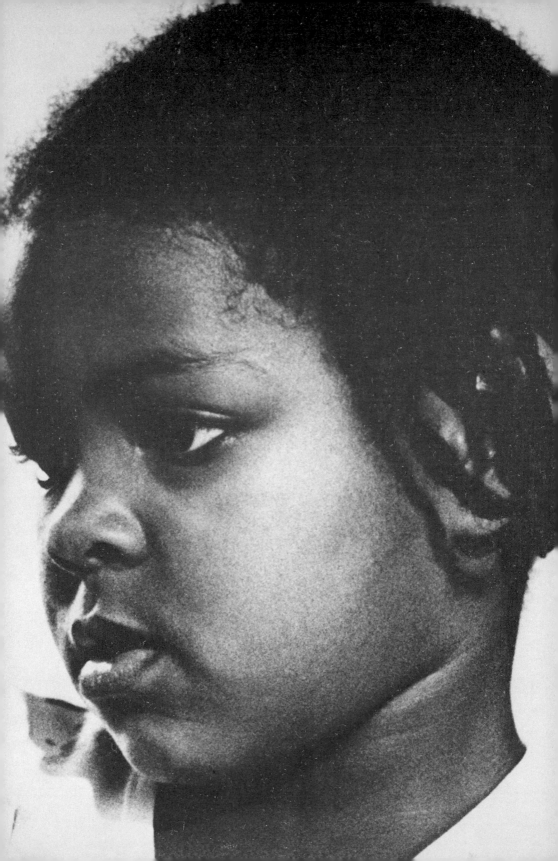

disgusted because Tommy does this so often. Kristy was angry because he really hurts her, and even if he didn't, it is very annoying. Tommy seems to be jealous of Kristy, because I noticed he did it right after I told her how nicely she had combed her hair."

   c. Restate the problem in as few words as possible on the basis of your answers to items a and b; for example, "Tommy annoys Kristy frequently by poking her in the ribs. I think he's jealous of her."

   d. Determine how often this or a similar situation happens. In the above example, the answer would be "It happens several times a day, usually when I am paying specific attention to Kristy."

2. Narrow down exactly who and what are immediately affected by the problem; for example, "(1) Tommy, (2) myself, (3) Kristy."

3. State what you think is the possible cause of the problem. For example, is it:

   a. Genetic? (Considering the situation with Kristy and Tommy, the answer is no.)

   b. Developmental or perceptual? (Kristy is much more capable at perceptual motor tasks than is Tommy; she has greater self-esteem.)

   c. Educational? (No.)

   d. Cultural? (No.)

   e. Social environment? (Kristy has many playmates in the neighborhood. There are no boys nearby for Tommy to play with. The girls often don't want him to play with them.)

   f. Physical environment? (He seems to have some hay fever which often makes him feel uncomfortable.)

4. Specify the change you want to effect. For example, "I want Tommy to have greater self-esteem, stop being so jealous of his sister, and stop poking her in the ribs all the time."

5. Define limitations to making a change. (The purpose of this is to eliminate the possibility of excuses.) Is there a lack of time? Cooperation? Professional help? Knowledge? Money?

6. Specify exactly what you need and must do to make the change. The following would apply in Tommy's case:

    a. Time: set one month as a goal.

    b. Energy: yours and your husband's.

    c. Cooperation: relatives and friends who visit.

    d. Professional help: allergy specialist.

    e. Communication: keep diary of progress.

    f. More knowledge: about children's feelings, sibling rivalry, and jealousy. Read books, talk to psychologist friend.

    g. Money: the cost of the allergy specialist needs to be considered. Insurance will cover most of the expenses.

    h. Anticipate the emotional cost of the effort: this method of problem solving takes determination, understanding, persistence, and empathy. Be prepared to bolster each other's spirits as you and your spouse remain determined to carry out your plan.

7. Taking the preceding steps into account, design a plan for change.

    a. Set up a timetable. For example:
        Week one. Have allergy tests done. Keep a diary of all incidents between Kristy and Tommy. Give Tommy compliments. Spend time with Tommy. Avoid complimenting Kristy in front of Tommy.

Week two. Analyze diary with spouse. Try to pinpoint those factors which seem to trigger Tommy's actions against Kristy. Continue with allergist.

Week three. Implement changes as indicated by diary and as result of allergy tests.

Week four. Evaluate. Make further plans if needed.

b. List people who will be involved: In this case, Kristy, Tommy, mother, father, doctor (also, friends).

c. Keep a step-by-step record of your implementation of the plan.

d. Continually review the record of the plan. Modify it as necessary.

When the problem being worked on has been lessened, or the behavior has been modified or changed, you will probably realize that it is due to your own changed attitudes and actions.

What You Have Learned

If you have been practicing the "magic list" alternatives to punitive discipline, you have learned to approach your parental responsibility from a more professional viewpoint. You have learned that it is all right to express anger, as long as you are in control of that anger. You have learned that the discipline of your children is no more than the development of a wholesome, caring system of interpersonal relationships based on treating them as you would want to be treated if you were in their place.

You have learned that you can prevent many problems in these relationships by following some simple guidelines of being assertive, positive, clear in your expectations, flexible, and caring. You have learned that you can often prevent discipline problems from arising, if you anticipate such problems and apply a problem-prevention technique such as giving reminders, distracting, injecting humor, or offering choices. Establishing good habits of communication, giving praise or compliments, offering encouragement, and clarifying messages also help prevent problems. You have learned the value of showing restraint by overlooking small annoyances and by reconsidering the situations arising that seem to surface discipline problems. You have learned the value of pointing out natural or logical consequences in a positive, nonpunitive manner, and of substituting a positive renewal time for a punitive "time-out." You've learned the magic of using hugs and caring as a disciplinary measure and the importance of avoiding arguments by teaching children the art of discussion. You've been introduced to a method of self-help problem solving that has been used successfully by hundreds of parents.

Most of all, you have learned that by walking gently, hand in hand with your children, together you will grow.

A Selected Bibliography

You may find the following books helpful for further pursuit of some of the questions raised in this book.

Baruch, Dorothy W. *New Ways in Discipline*. New York: McGraw-Hill, 1949. An early book on humanistic discipline, it emphasizes the legitimacy of allowing children the privilege of expressing true feelings. Out-of-print. Obtain through public library.

Bessell, Harold, and Thomas P. Kelly, Jr. *The Parent Book: The Holistic Program for Raising the Emotionally Mature Child*. San Diego: Psych/Graphic Publishers, 1977. An excellent guide to the emotional development of children and how the emotions can be responded to constructively to minimize conflict between parents and their children. I highly recommend this book.

Cherry, Clare. *Creative Movement for the Developing Child: A Handbook for Non-Musicians*. Belmont, CA: David S. Lake Publishers (formerly Pitman Learning), 1971. A very basic introduction to the perceptual-motor development of children and to sensory-motor integrative activities. Written for teachers, but useful to parents of infants and toddlers.

––––––. *Think of Something Quiet: A Guide to Serenity in the Classroom*. Belmont, CA: David S. Lake Publishers, 1981. Suggests that the establishment of a humanistic program built around an environment and curriculum geared toward stress reduction can reduce the frequency of conflict with children. Written for teachers, but equally useful to parents.

Dodson, Fitzhugh. *How to Discipline—with Love*. New York: New American Library, 1978. This book presents discipline as teaching. Taking the age of the child into account, Dodson stresses that there can be no overall formula for teaching desirable behavior but rather a wide variety of flexible, practical strategies to draw from according to each individual situation—a humane approach that stresses the importance of love and rapport as ongoing elements of interpersonal relationships with children. However, This book is very sexist.

Dreikurs, Rudolf, M.D. *Coping with Children's Misbehavior: A Parents Guide*. New York: Hawthorn 1972. This book stresses the importance of investigating the reasons behind children's misbehavior.

––––––. and Vicki Soltz. *Children: The Challenge*. New York: Hawthorn, 1964. This book is based on Dreikurs's system of natural consequences in dealing with discipline.

Faber, Adele, and Elaine Mazlish. *How to Talk so Kids Will Listen and Listen so Kids Will Talk.* New York: Rawson, Wade, 1980. This book emphasizes the differences between helpful and unhelpful methods of communication, and is geared toward the reduction of conflicts and tensions between parents and their children.

Fraiberg, Selma. *The Magic Years.* New York: Scribner's, 1959. Fraiberg suggests gearing disciplinary practices to the understanding of what can be expected of children at their various levels of maturity. She feels that, rather than punishment, children need help, understanding, and a great deal of emotional support. This book is especially valuable for the understanding of the needs of infants and toddlers as they try to master their environment.

Ginott, Haim. *Between Parent and Child: New Solutions to Old Problems.* New York: Macmillan, 1965. (Also Avon paperback.) Ginott writes about communication between parents and their children, giving guidelines to conveyance of self-respect and positive feelings even when giving statements of advice, correction, or instruction. He emphasizes the validity of reflecting children's feelings.

Gordon, Thomas. *Parent Effectiveness Training: The Tested New Way to Raise Responsible Children.* New York: Peter H. Wyden, 1970. (Also available in paperback.) Addresses the importance of humanistic attitudes when dealing with family conflicts, utilizing the communication of feelings to solve problems.

Klein, Carole. *How It Feels to Be a Child.* New York: Harper and Row, 1975. Dispels the myth of an always happy childhood and opens doors to understanding the fears, anxieties, loneliness, and other problems of children's inner feelings.

Peairs, Lillian, and Richard H. Peairs. *What Every Child Needs.* New York: Harper and Row, 1974. An excellent book for parents who are seeking to raise emotionally healthy children. Contains excellent chapters on anger and hostility and on keys to better discipline. A helpful book for teachers, too, and for teenage brothers and sisters of younger children.

Index